Root Scaling and Planing

A Fundamental Therapy

Bernard Wasserman, D.D.S.
Clinical Professor of Periodontics
School of Dental and Oral Surgery
Columbia University
New York, New York

Quintessence Publishing Co., Inc. 1986
Chicago, London, Berlin, São Paulo and Tokyo

The original Japanese edition was published under the title *Color Atlas: Scaling and Root Planing* by Quintessence Publishing Co., Ltd., Tokyo, in 1984.

Library of Congress Cataloging-in-Publication Data

Wasserman, Bernard.
 Root scaling and planing.

 Includes bibliographies and index.
 1. Dental scaling.   2. Teeth—Roots—Planing.
I. Title. [DNLM: 1. Dental Prophylaxis.   2. Tooth Root—
surgery. WU 113 W322v]
RK60.75.S27W37   1986   617.6′34   86-3194
ISBN 0-86715-177-3

© 1986 by Quintessence Publishing Co., Inc., Chicago, Illinois.

Lithography: Sun Art Printing Co., Osaka
Composition: The Clarinda Co., Clarinda IA
Printing and binding: Franz W. Wesel Druckerei und Verlag GmbH & Co. KG., Baden-Baden

Printed in West Germany 130897

Dedication

To my wife, Evelyn, whose support was unending.

Contents

Chapter 1   Variation in Health and Disease   11

Chapter 2   Objectives of Definitive Deep Scaling   39

Chapter 3   Predictable Results from Definitive Deep Scaling   49

Chapter 4   Instruments for Scaling and Planing   63

Chapter 5   Instrument Maintenance   76

Chapter 6   Root Scaling and Planing Techniques   84

Chapter 7   Areas of Difficulty   113

Chapter 8   Pain Control   121

Chapter 9   Choice and Sequence of Treatment   124

Chapter 10   Maintenance Phase   137

Chapter 11   Case Reports   143

Index   158

Preface

This volume is a guide to the theory and techniques of deep scaling and root planing for the treatment of periodontal disease. Because of the observed long-term success of clinical results, deep scaling and root planing have become the cornerstones for successful periodontal therapy and prevention of recurrence.

Although results vary from case to case, controlled clinical studies have suggested that treatment of periodontal disease by deep scaling and root planing on the average produces results comparable to those of other treatment modalities. For long-term maintenance, however, case reports unequivocally establish the importance of deep scaling in this essential treatment phase.

Both the immediate and long-term results of periodontal therapies are closely related to the responses of the periodontal tissues to the etiologic agents present. This book stresses analyzing these variations in the clinical signs and symptoms of periodontal disease so that practitioners' decisions to use deep scaling and root planing for treatment will be based on accurate prognoses. Anatomic variations that affect the disease process and its clinical manifestations are shown. In addition, the strengths and limitations of deep scaling and root planing are carefully described. With an understanding of such clinical interrelations the practitioner can better diagnose the disease, prescribe the most efficacious therapy, and establish realistic clinical endpoints to treatment.

All techniques in this text are shown being executed in the two most common operator-patient positions. The comprehensive section on instrument design should lead to a wider understanding of instrument choice and use. The descriptions of the utilization of a greater variety of instruments provide the practitioner with choices frequently lacking in texts on periodontal treatment. Unique to periodontal literature are the text's diagrams suggesting direction of instrument use in shallow and deep pockets for each tooth surface.

This text contains both the carefully described theory and methodology that is required by trainees in periodontal therapy, and the diagnostic, therapeutic, and prognostic insights that are of such practical value to daily practitioners of dental hygiene, general dentistry, and periodontics.

Our special thanks go to Dr. K. Matsumoto, P. Wood, C. McDonald, and P. Sclafani.

Chapter 1

Variation in Health and Disease

The healthy periodontium

Since all periodontal therapy is directed at reestablishing health, it is important to establish a concept of the clinically normal periodontium. In the periodontium, as in all biology, variation within a normal range is the rule rather than the exception. The color of normal gingiva can vary from delicate pearly pink to deeper red and blue-black depending on pigmentation, vascularity, thickness, or the degree of keratinization. The gingiva can be relatively thin with a fine marginal edge adjacent to the tooth, or it may be thick with a heavy flat margin (Figs. 1-1a to d). The heavier the underlying alveolar bone, the thicker the marginal gingiva. Within a dentition, tooth prominence in the dental arch or a position lingual to adjacent teeth will determine gingival marginal thickness. The more prominent the tooth, the thinner the alveolar bone and gingiva (Figs. 1-2a to c). The most frequent surface characteristic of the gingiva is a fine stippling, with the surface stippling being somewhat less pronounced in the marginal free gingiva (Fig. 1-3). However, the gingiva may have surface textures ranging from that of an orange peel to that of a fine, velvetlike stippling, or it may have an almost smooth surface (Figs. 1-4a and b). The stippled gingiva has a keratinized epithelium.

The width of the attached stippled (keratinized) gingiva varies greatly between individuals and is usually narrower in the mandibular premolar and second molar regions within a dentition. Immediately apical to the attached gingiva is the freely movable gingival mucosa, which is elastic and has a nonkeratinized, thin epithelium. The mucogingival junction can be clinically delineated as the flexure line when the lip, cheek, or floor of the mouth is drawn occlusally (Figs. 1-5a and b). The labial and lingual frenula and occasional high muscle attachments modify the elasticity of the mucosa and may cause a narrowing of the attached gingiva by drawing it outward and downward with resultant gingival recession. On the palate the gingiva is continuous with the keratinized, fibrous, and fixed palatal mucosa.

The marginal gingiva extends into the proximal embrasures in the form of the pyramidal interdental papilla, which reaches occlusally to the contact point. Depending on the width of the contact point and the length of the crowns, a shallower or deeper interdental col exists running buccolingually in the papillae of posterior teeth (Fig. 1-6). In the absence of proximal tooth contact, the papilla flattens to form a small saddle area (Fig. 1-7).

Figs. 1-1a to d Variations in normal gingiva thickness, color, and surface texture.

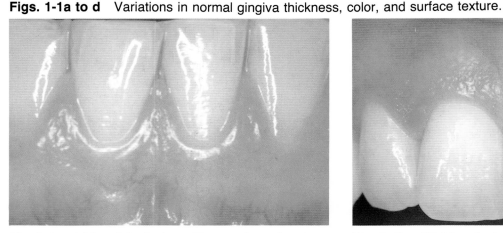

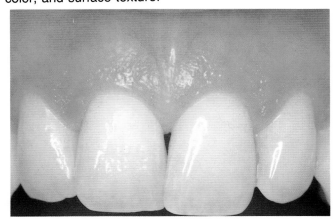

Fig. 1-1a Thin, pink gingiva with vascular extensions into stippled gingiva.

Fig. 1-1b Slight melanin pigmentation.

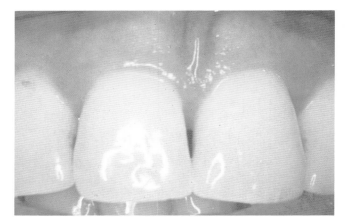

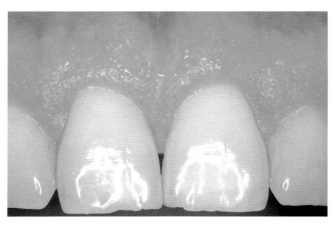

Fig. 1-1c Whitish pink gingiva.

Fig. 1-1d Thick, pink, fibrous gingiva with pebbled surface. The thinner the gingiva, the more obvious any inflammatory change in form. Similarly, the paler the color, the more apparent inflammatory color changes.

The marginal portion of keratinized gingiva is not attached to the tooth (the free gingiva) and forms the outer wall of the gingival sulcus. The epithelium of the sulcular surface of the free gingiva adjacent to the tooth is not keratinized. A groove in the facial gingiva, the free gingival groove, is frequently evident but only approximately delineates the depth of the gingival sulcus in normal gingiva. Immediately apical to the sulcus, the gingiva is attached to the tooth by the junctional epithelium. The junctional epithelium is biologically very active and acts as an ever-renewing source of cells for the epithelial attachment. It also allows transmigration of leukocytes and the pas-

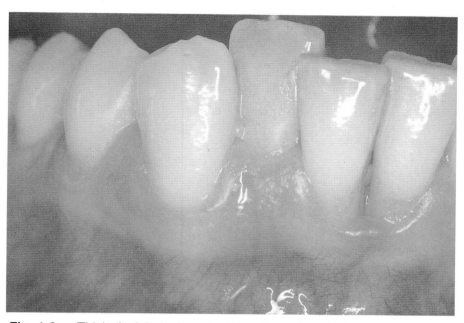

Fig. 1-2a Thick, facial gingiva of a lingually malposed lateral incisor tooth is normal. Attempts to thin the margin without changing tooth position would be futile. The prominent canine has a thin gingival margin and alveolar housing.

Fig. 1-2c Thick alveolar process with commensurate thicker marginal gingiva. Periodontal fiber detachment by disease would probably produce pockets and infrabony lesions.

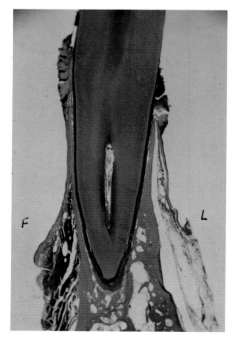

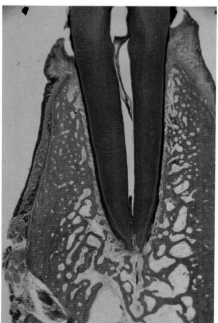

Fig. 1-2b Thin alveolar housing of an anterior tooth in a narrow alveolar process. Note both facial and lingual surfaces are thin. In disease the total alveolar process would be lost, producing recession rather than a pocket, as evident on the lingual surface.

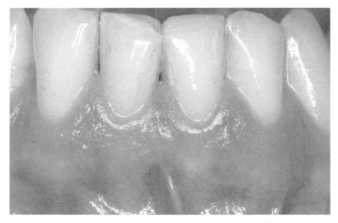

Fig. 1-3 Finely stippled normal gingiva. Stippling is less pronounced in the marginal portion.

Figs. 1-4a and b Variations in surface stippling of normal gingiva.

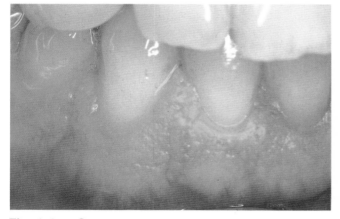

Fig. 1-4a Orange-peel surface.

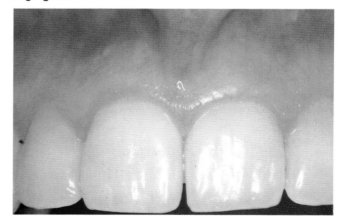

Fig. 1-4b Near absence of stippling. Loss of stippling, an early sign of inflammation, must be gauged by the previous degree of stippling in the normal gingiva of a given patient.

sage of substance with moderately large molecules in both directions. More apically, the gingiva is attached to the root cementum by collagen fibers, first to the root surface and then to the periosteum of the alveolar bone (Fig. 1-8). Alveolar bone thickness is highly variable within dentitions and between individuals, predisposing to differences in the patterns and morphology of pathologic changes.

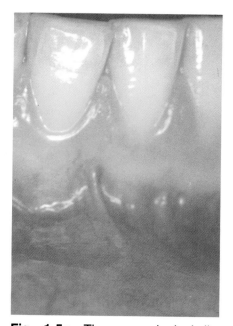

Fig. 1-5a The mucogingival line, determined by drawing the lip upward and outward, is the apical limit of the attached gingiva. Very narrow zones of attached gingiva may sometimes associate with ease of pocket formation on prominent roots.

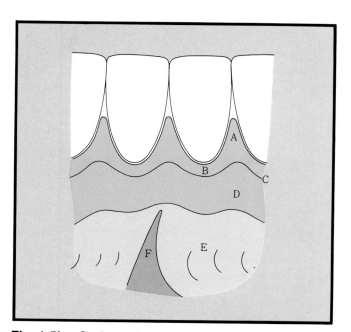

Fig. 1-5b Surface characteristics of the gingiva: A = gingival papilla; B = marginal gingiva; C = free gingival groove; D = attached gingiva; E = alveolar mucosa; F = labial frenum.

Fig. 1-6 The interdental col, or depression, in the normal gingival papilla as viewed from the proximal surface reflects the width of the tooth contact area and the gingival height. The wider the contact area, the wider the col; the higher the gingiva on the crown, the deeper the col. The col is an area susceptible to inflammation and therefore early disease.

Fig. 1-7 Interdental saddle areas or flattened papillae in areas of diastemata between teeth are less susceptible to disease than the col area.

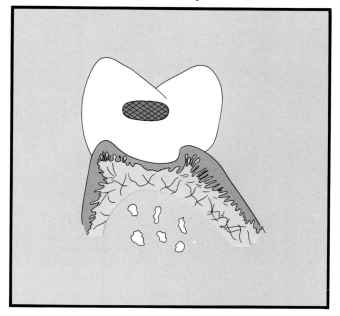

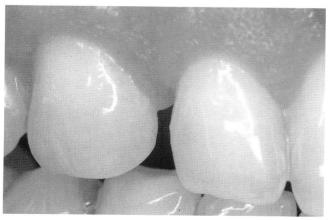

Variation in Health and Disease

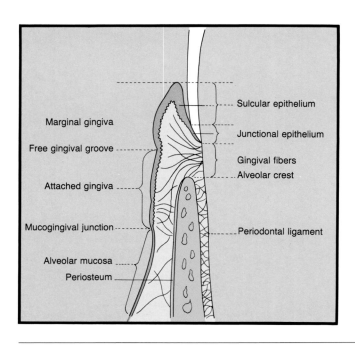

Fig. 1-8 Normal gingiva and periodontium in cross section, indicating associated surface area desginations.

Development of plaque and calculus

Freshly cleaned tooth surfaces quickly develop an organic dental pellicle as salivary proteins adhere to the mineral surfaces. Bacteria colonize the surface in small numbers and begin to proliferate. At this time no visible dental plaque is evident. Staining with disclosing solution would produce only very light and uniform staining of the tooth surface. The bacterial colonies rapidly enlarge, coalesce, and finally develop into a visibly thickened dental plaque. In uncleaned areas the bacterial plaque overgrows, with a concomitant change in bacterial flora, from one predominantly made up of Gram-positive cocci and rods, to one with more Gram-negative rods, motile bacteria, and spirochetes. Gingival inflammation seems to be initiated by these late-colonizing Gram-negative and motile organisms. There is no doubt that bacteria are primary etiologic agents in most forms of periodontal disease, as evidenced in both experimental and epidemiologic studies. However, gingival inflammation can result from other local causes, a most frequent one being the drying of the gingival surfaces due to mouth breathing. Similarly, gingival inflammation is found in those syndromes associated with reduced salivary flow, such as postradiation salivary insufficiency.

Marginal gingival surfaces in contact with bacterial plaque accumulations will develop the signs of gingival inflammation. These signs consist of gingival color changes, ranging from red to cyanotic as a result of vascular enlargement and stasis, and are associated with gingival bleeding. Ease of retraction of the gingival margins from the teeth as well as size and contour changes are due to edema and the infiltration of inflammatory cells. The interdental papillae in general are more susceptible to inflammation because of their greater area of surface contact relative to tissue volume and difficulty in

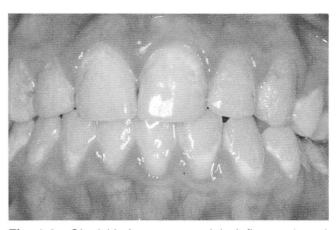

Fig. 1-9 Gingivitis in a young adult. Inflammation of the interdental papillae is a frequent first change from normal.

proximal surface plaque removal (Fig. 1-9). The original thickness and fibrous tissue content of the gingiva as well as the inherent tendency of the individual to a more or less exudative inflammatory reaction will modify the appearance of the affected gingiva. In some instances only a very local response in the form of a thin, bright red, smooth-surfaced line at the gingival margins will be present. In the range of responses, at one extreme, the tissue may be highly proliferative with extreme inflammatory enlargement and cyanosis; at the other extreme only slight gingival contour and color change may occur. The inflammation may be localized to the margin or may extend through the whole width of stippled gingiva (Figs. 1-10a to g).

The gingival tissue, having undergone an inflammatory enlargement, causes an increase in gingival pocket depth. Such a gingival pocket can be expected to be eliminated by the reduction of inflammation and must be differentiated from a true periodontal pocket, which is in part the result of detachment of the periodontal fibers from the cementum (Fig. 1-11).

Concurrent with bacterial plaque extension into the deepened gingival sulcus and into every irregularity of the tooth surface, dental calculus forms. First the noncellular matrix of the plaque calcifies, followed by calcification within the organisms, and finally inclusion of the microorganisms within the expanding calculus mass. Viable organisms extend outward from the calculus surface as part of both the supragingival and subgingival plaque.

As the gingival inflammation extends through and around the transseptal periodontal fibers and approaches the alveolar crest, the alveolar bone undergoes remodeling with bone resorption and, to a lesser degree, reactive bone formation. The attachment of the gingival fibers is lost to both tooth and alveolar bone. The junctional epithelium proliferates into the previous area of gingival fiber attach-

Variation in Health and Disease

Figs. 1-10a and b Slight to moderately reactive patient.

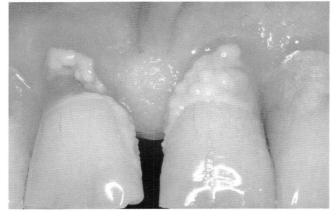

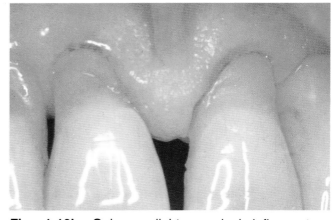

Fig. 1-10a Plaque accumulation caused by inadequate brushing during a 5-week period.

Fig. 1-10b Only a slight marginal inflammatory change is evident. The degree of inflammation is a characteristic of individual patient responses.

ment, the more coronal epithelium separates from the tooth, and the sulcus deepens. The space occupied by bacterial plaque is now called a *periodontal pocket,* and the clinical description changes from gingivitis to periodontitis (Figs. 1-12a and b and 1-13a and b).

Developmental stages of periodontal disease

To more readily conceptualize the disease process, the histologic changes that occur in the sequence from health to disease have been divided into stages of development.

1. Clinically healthy gingival tissue usually has very small areas of less dense collagen tissue adjacent to the junctional epithelium. Lymphocytes and monocytes in these lightly infiltrated areas represent the major cellular component. Polymorphonuclear leukocytes and plasma cells in combination account for less than 10% of the cell population. Absolute health with no gingival infiltrate is rarely found, though it can be produced by repeated scalings and extremely meticulous plaque control for several weeks.

2. The initial gingival lesion, resulting from plaque accumulation and maturation, includes cellular and vascular changes. There is an increase in the vascular bed by dilation of existing vessels and blood vessel configuration changes, as well as greater small vessel permeability. The area of less dense collagen increases, with local collagen fiber loss of 60% to 70%. The cellular infiltrate has characteristics of an acute inflammatory reaction with larger numbers of polymorphonuclear leukocytes and monocyte/macrophages associated with

Figs. 1-10c and d Nonreactive patient who exhibits little or no clinical inflammation with disease.

Fig. 1-10c Heavy supragingival calculus accumulated over a 4-month period.

Fig. 1-10d The gingiva exhibited no visible inflammation immediately after calculus removal.

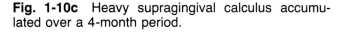

Fig. 1-10e Thick gingiva masking localized gingival inflammation associated with a pocket distal to the canine.

Fig. 1-10g Marginal periodontitis with both fibrous and inflammatory gingival thickening. A general cyanosis of the tissue is evident. This tissue is less responsive to deep scaling.

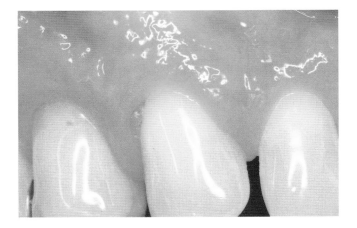

Fig. 1-10f Marginal inflammation of a proliferative, highly vascular nature extending through the attached gingiva in the central incisor area. This tissue is more responsive to deep scaling.

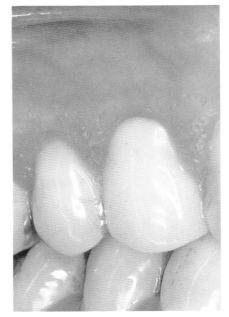

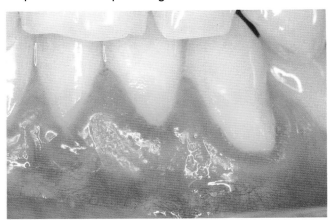

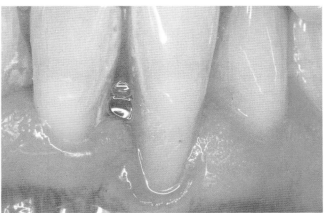

lesser numbers of lymphocytes. Considerable numbers of polymorpho-nuclear leukocytes traversing the junctional epithelium are evident. The lymphocytes infiltrating the connective tissue are primarily of the T-cell (thymus-derived) variety, possibly indicating a concurrent delayed hypersensitivity immunologic response. This acute pathologic phase is transient and rapidly undergoes change to a more chronic inflammatory reaction or reversal to normal.

3. The early lesion exhibits somewhat more extensive areas of infiltrated connective tissue associated with some proliferation of the sulcular epithelium in the form of rete pegs. The same variety of inflammatory cells is present, though lesser numbers of polymorpho-nuclear leukocytes are present in the inflamed connective tissue. The lymphocyte population includes a higher percentage of B cells, which are precursors of antibody-producing plasma cells. Fibroblasts decrease in number and exhibit degenerative changes, a condition that may possibly contribute to the reduced collagen content of the inflamed area.

4. The established gingival lesion exhibits further extension of the infiltrated collagen-poor connective tissue. There are changes in the proportions of the cellular components of the infiltrate; the lymphocytes decrease, and the plasma cells and immunologically differentiating blast cells increase. The lymphocytes are primarily of the B-cell type as opposed to a previously predominant T-cell population. From an immunologic viewpoint, it is hypothesized that the delayed hypersensitivity immunologic response mediated by T cells is now converted to primarily a humoral response mediated by B-lymphocytes and plasma cells. Ulcerations and extensive rete peg proliferations as well as thinning of the sulcular epithelium are evident.

5. In the advanced lesion, epithelial downgrowth and pocket formation occur. The direction of change in cell populations continues as plasma cells and blast cells increase and lymphocytes and fibroblasts decrease when compared with the established gingival lesion. The amount of collagen remaining in the inflamed area decreases to approximately one fourth the amount found in the near healthy gingiva. The prevalence of cell-associated immunoglobulin indicates that the local immunologic response is primarily humoral. Locally produced antibodies to bacteria in the sulcus are found in the crevicular fluid. It is possible that a cell-mediated hypersensitivity reaction persists even in advanced lesions since 7% of the lymphocyte population is the T-cell type. These cells probably also have a helping and mediating function in relation to B-cell activity.

The biologic mechanisms that produce the histopathologic changes in the gingiva have not been accurately defined. However, in Fig. 1-14 the complexity of the local environment of the gingival sulcus and a number of experimentally substantiated tissue reactions within the gingiva are graphically represented. The bacteria are the primary etiologic agents and can affect tissue by producing enzymes such as hyaluronidase, which increases tissue permeability to toxic agents such as bacterial endotoxin and bacterial metabolites.

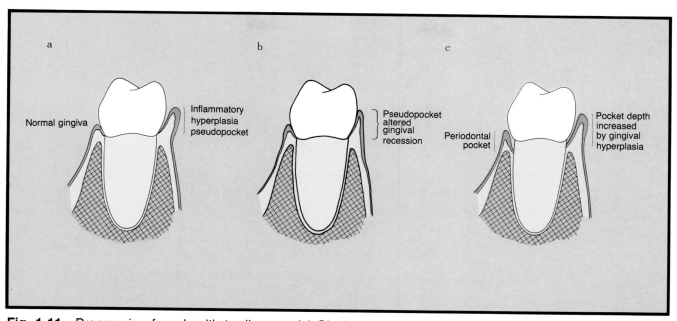

Fig. 1-11 Progression from health to disease: *(a)* Gingival inflammation enlargement produces a pseudoperiodontal pocket since no periodontal fibers have detached from the root. The pocket depth is a function of the degree of gingival inflammatory hyperplasia and will be easily reduced by deep scaling. *(b)* An altered passive eruption (absence of normal recession of the gingiva after tooth eruption) produces a pseudopocket on the lingual side of many mandibular molars that will remain after deep scaling. *(c)* Equal loss of attachment on both facial and lingual sides. The lingual pocket depth measurement will be greater, reflecting the gingival inflammatory hyperplasia.

Fig. 1-12a Clinically evident inflammatory hyperplasia of the gingiva with enlargement, color change, loss of stippling, and pocket depth.

Fig. 1-12b Histopathologic section of the hyperplastic papilla between teeth 6 and 7 in Fig. 1-12a. Note highly vascular, densely infiltrated gingiva with almost no collagen fibers remaining within the area of inflammation. Courtesy of Dr. B. Moskow.

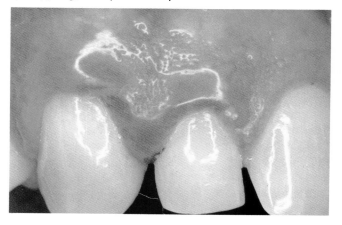

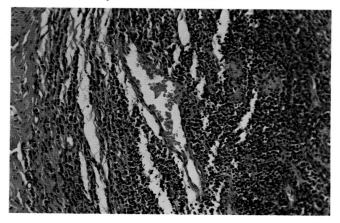

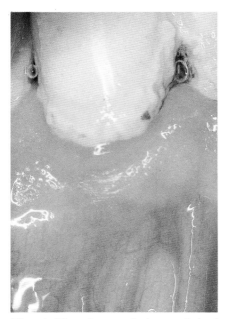

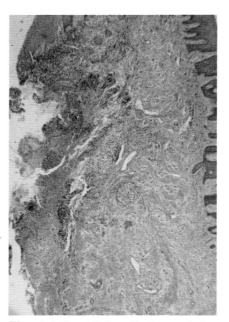

Fig. 1-13a Less obvious clinical inflammation of the gingiva overlying a periodontal pocket. Except for a slight cyanosis, the thick gingiva appears relatively normal in spite of heavy plaque accumulation and represents a nonreactive gingival response.

Fig. 1-13b Histopathology of the thick, nonresponsive tissues in Fig. 1-13a. Note the area of inflammatory exudate is localized to the subsulcular tissue. The great mass of collagen fibers in the gingiva is intact. The fiber destruction is limited to the area adjacent to the tooth without massive inflammatory changes. Note extreme difference in response compared with the patient in Figs. 1-12a and b.

Complex substances of bacterial origin may act as antigens to which the immunocompetent cells of the gingiva induce a delayed hypersensitivity reaction as well as specific antibodies. Such antibodies, by reacting with antigen, activate the complex complement system, which then amplifies a series of destructive reactions. The bacteria, as well as elements of the complement system, are chemotactic to leukocytes, which may then release tissue-destructive lysozomal enzymes during phagocytosis and cell death. Antigens may also cause sensitized lymphocytes to undergo blastogenesis, with production of such biologically active lymphokines as osteoclast activation factor and kinins that cause vascular dilation, proliferation, increased permeability, and direct and indirect cytotoxic actions. Prostaglandins capable of inducing vascular changes and osteoclasis are activated by bacterial metabolites and tissue injury. The possibilities for tissue alteration and destruction are numerous and easily account

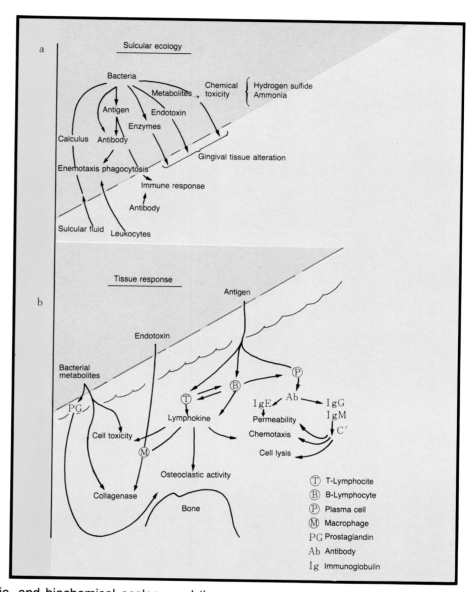

Fig. 1-14 The organismic, biologic, and biochemical ecology and tissue response of the gingival sulcus: *(a)* Bacterial plaque undergoes calcification as a result of complex processes in which the calcium and phosphate of gingival fluid are precipitated. Leukocytes engulf bacteria and in the process liberate destructive lysosomal enzymes. Bacterial plaque, chemotactic to leukocytes, causes migration of leukocytes into the sulcus. Bacterial antigens react with antibodies of the gingival fluid and activate the complement system. Antigens penetrate the gingiva, are absorbed by macrophages, and initate an immune reaction in the immunoactive cells of the gingiva. Enzymes, endotoxins, and direct-acting chemical agents lyse and destroy components of the gingival tissues. *(b)* The gingival tissues and alveolar bone may undergo numerous changes that result from the immune response to bacterial antigen. In addition, prostaglandins produced by epithelium cells can activate osteoclasts that may destroy alveolar bone. Macrophages produce a collagenase when activated. Delayed hypersensitivity reactions involve T-lymphocyte, whereas B cells react to bacterial antigens. Both produce lymphokines with various biologic activity as indicated. Plasma cells resulting from B-lymphocyte transformation produce antibodies that then react with locally present antigens. The antigen-antibody complexes initiate the multiactive complement system.

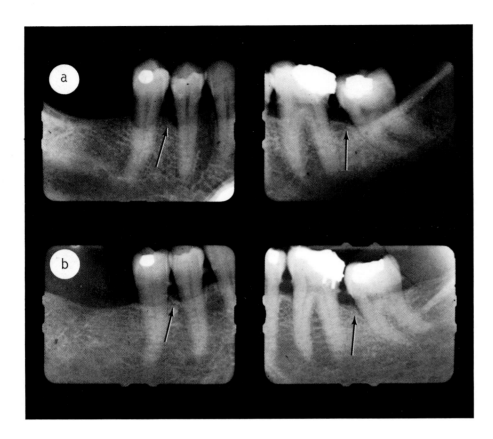

Fig. 1-15 Radiographs of a patient with advanced disease who refused treatment: *(a)* periodontal destruction in 1965, *(b)* little if any further destruction evident in 1975 in spite of lack of treatment. Courtesy of Dr. B. Moskow.

for the histopathologic changes. The defense mechanisms of the body, which counter the effect of organisms in the gingival sulcus and soft tissue wall of the pocket, include phagocytozing polymorphonuclear leukocytes and macrophages assisted by the opsonins produced by immunoactive cells. A variety of homeostatic and feedback mechanisms (e.g., α antitrypsin and α macroglobulin, which inhibit elastase and collagenase activity) operate to limit tissue destruction.

The clinical implications of this general description of the progression of periodontal disease from gingivitis to periodontitis are misleading, however. Indeed, many areas of gingivitis never progress beyond that stage, even in dentitions where further periodontal destruction and pocketing is occurring elsewhere. There is usually a wide range of tissue reactivity and defensive capacity within an individual dentition and in compared dentitions. As an unusual example of the balance between destructive factors and individual host resistance, Fig. 1-15 illustrates an advanced periodontal case, which after ten years with no treatment exhibited no further periodontal destruction. Some studies of nonsurgically treated cases indicate that little or no advancement of disease occurs in many unreachable furca-

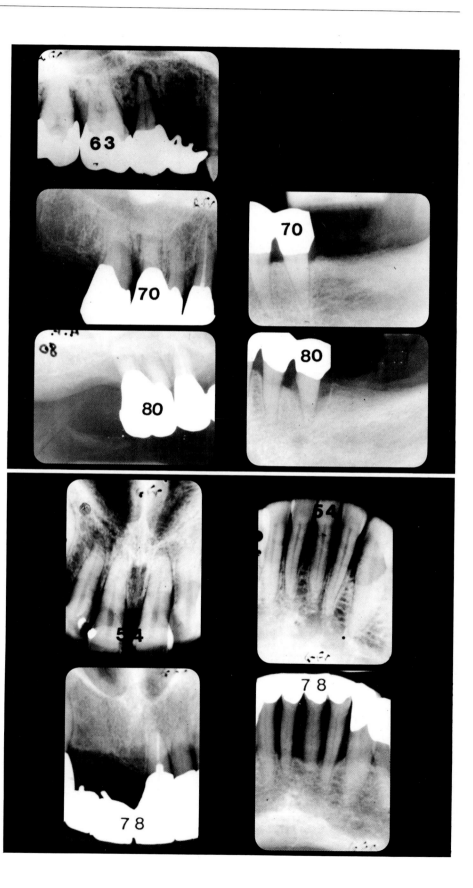

Fig. 1-16a Cyclic active destruction in a downhill case. Area at onset (1963) had severe destruction. Note periapical bone and crestal fill (1970). Posttreatment loss of filled crestal bone. Further loss of alveolar support. Note new deep lesion on lower premolar (1980).

Fig. 1-16b Progressive downhill case that exhibited little gingival inflammation.

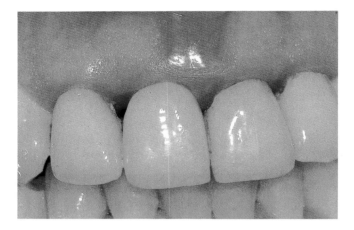

Fig. 1-17 Thick, fibrous gingiva masks underlying pathologic inflammatory changes that might be overlooked during cursory examination. Pockets of 5 to 6 mm were present about most teeth.

tion-involved molars during long-term maintenance. This fact suggests that stability of some treated cases may represent a state of remission of disease activity rather than success related to therapy. In the majority of cases, however, for some periodontally diseased areas the tendency is toward further destruction when left untreated. Long-term studies consistently indicate that loss of periodontal attachment is significantly slowed or halted by treatment.

Though the highly susceptible individual will progressively lose periodontal attachment and bone, with ultimate tooth loss, the process is by no means a continuous and constantly advancing one. Periods of active local destruction, general remission, and even repair occur (Fig. 1-16a). In other very susceptible individuals, random active destruction may occur in a step-wise fashion (Fig. 1-16b). It has been postulated that changes in the virulence or composition of the subgingival microflora account for these variations. Though the microflora are undoubtedly primary elements in the progress of disease, major modifying factors must exist to explain the usual bilateral symmetry of disease as well as single arch susceptibilities frequently observed.

A wide range of clinical signs can be associated in periodontal disease. It follows, therefore, that the amount of gingival inflammation in a case of periodontitis may or may not correlate well with pocket depth. Inflammation-induced color and contour changes in the gingiva overlying a periodontal pocket are frequently but not always visible. Where the gingiva is thick and fibrous or the alveolar process is wide, the inflammation within the pocket wall is masked by the overlying fibrous tissue or bone. When such pockets are probed, bleeding usually occurs because of the vascular, inflamed tissue below the ulcerated sulcular epithelium (Fig. 1-17). Gingiva of average thickness overlying a pocket may appear cyanotic through-

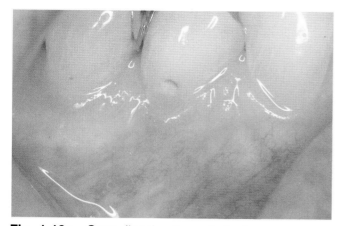

Fig. 1-18a Gray discoloration of gingiva represents subgingival calculus visible through the gingiva.

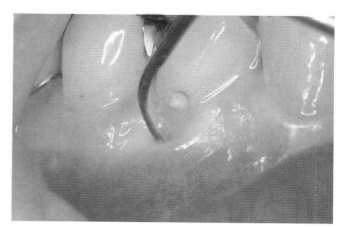

Fig. 1-18b Retraction of the gingiva to expose underlying calculus.

out, indicating a diffuse infiltrate in the gingiva. A gray discoloration of thin gingiva usually indicates underlying subgingival calculus (Figs. 1-18a and b). A small group of patients exhibit little or no gingival inflammation in the presence of deep pockets. Patients with nonresponsive gingiva are among those who frequently experience extensive destruction during long-term maintenance.

Bacteria in periodontal disease

In health, the organisms associated with the gingival sulcus are limited in number and tend to be primarily Gram-positive and require an aerobic environment. On the other hand, organisms associated with gingivitis represent a bacterial proliferation that usually includes Gram-negative cocci, filamentous forms, flagellates, and spirochetes. Anaerobic bacteria, such as *Fusobacterium nucleatum* and *Bacteroides melaninogenicus* ssp. *intermedius,* are also present. As the lesion progresses toward periodontitis, the subgingival environment becomes organized and is relatively independent of the supragingival ecosystem. For example, good oral hygiene procedures instituted after pocket formation will have little effect on the subgingival flora or disease activity.

The subgingival organisms of adult periodontitis are varied from individual to individual and from site to site in a dentition. The composition of plaque is highly complex. Morphologically, a fixed portion is attached to the tooth and calculus surfaces, and a nonadherent portion is near the base of the sulcus and adjacent to the soft tissue side. As one passes from supragingival to subgingival plaque, the thick palisaded filamentous organisms of the attached layer of supra-

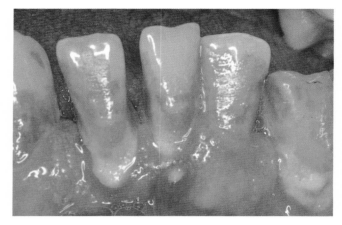

Fig. 1-19 Heavy supragingival calculus deposition mechanically causing gingival recession on right central incisor. Gingival inflammation and perforation on left central incisor related to heavy subgingival plaque and calculus.

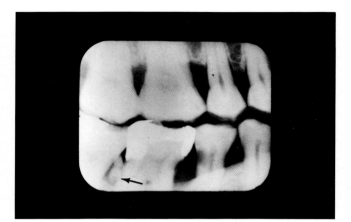

Fig. 1-20 Massive subgingival deposit that caused a soft tissue crater between teeth 30 and 31.

gingival plaque gives way to a thinner attached layer consisting of smaller bacteria, which have a more random arrangement. A nonadherent portion of the plaque between the adherent plaque and the soft tissue wall has flagellated organisms, some forming bristle-brush configurations with smaller Gram-negative fusiform bacteria. In addition, spirochetes, curved flagellated organisms, small coccoid forms, and Gram-negative rods are also present. The nonadherent plaque organisms produce more endotoxins than those of the adherent plaque. The layer of plaque closest to the soft tissue wall is lined with polymorphonuclear leukocytes and macrophages containing phagosomes with engulfed bacteria. *Bacteroides* seems to be most consistently associated with postjuvenile and adult periodontitis, though many other organisms are usually isolated, including *Eikenella, Viellonella, Fusobacterium, Selenomonas, Capnocytophaga,* and *Wolinella.* It would appear that the bacterial infection is of the mixed variety.

The laboratory techniques for isolation of subgingival organisms have become very sophisticated, and it is claimed that 90% of these organisms can be isolated and identified. Since some organisms, such as spirochetes, are difficult to grow in culture, and since they represent as much as 20% of the plaque, inherent deficiencies in the method are yet to be overcome. Newly identified isolates are frequent. In addition, the complexity of the techniques limit the number of sites that can be studied, limiting the value of the conclusions drawn. The specific organism or the combination of organisms that are the pathogens for periodontal diseases have yet to be defined.

The plaque of a normal sulcus becomes progressively more anaerobic and Gram-negative as the disease advances. Concurrently, the total number of organisms, as well as the percentage of motile forms, increases. In terms of therapy, once the subgingival plaque is

Figs. 1-21a and b Juvenile periodontitis (periodontosis) in a 15-year-old girl.

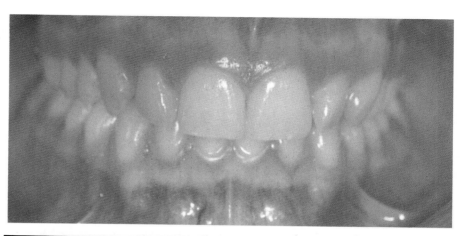

Fig. 1-21a Note noninflamed condition of the gingiva.

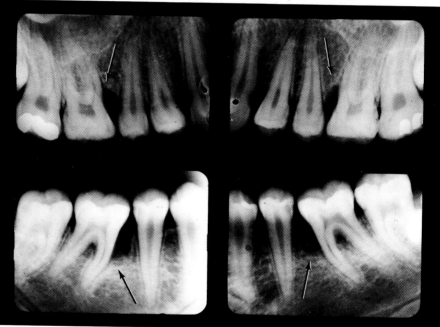

Fig. 1-21b Symmetric bone loss around the first molars is characteristic.

removed by deep scaling, the subgingival flora takes longer to reestablish itself than does supragingival plaque.

The relative role of subgingival calculus in the pathogenesis of periodontal disease is not clear. Since the presence of subgingival plaque precedes the development of subgingival calculus, one must conclude that bacterial plaque is the primary etiologic agent inducing the inflammation of periodontal disease. The role of subgingival calculus as an etiologic agent is most probably of secondary importance. Calculus is formed first as microcrystals within the plaque and thus is a latecomer to the environment. The roughness and irregular shape of the calculus provide a larger area for colonization by the bacteria and an increased area of contact with the pocket wall. This

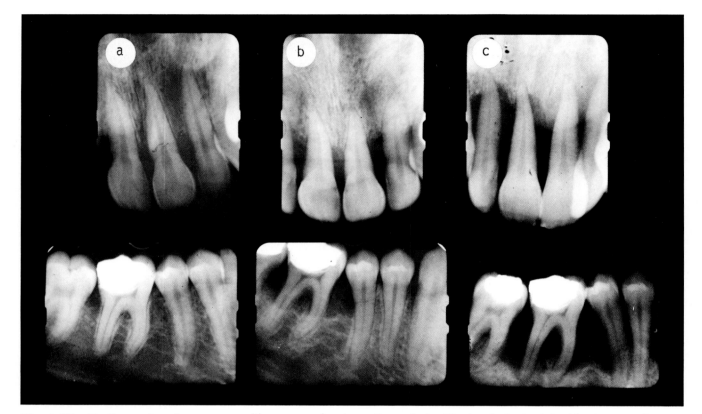

Fig. 1-22 Radiographs of a woman with progressive juvenile periodontitis (periodontosis) with changes from a localized to a disseminated type: *(a)* age 16, *(b)* age 20, *(c)* age 26.

greater contact and consequent greater mechanical and chemical irritation logically seem to be the mechanism for any increment in pathology attributable to calculus. In some instances, calculus deposition is so heavy that it becomes an etiologic agent because of its size. Thus, local facial or lingual gingival atrophy and soft tissue interdental craters may result from massive calculus deposition (Figs. 1-19 and 1-20). From a therapeutic viewpoint, any calculus remaining after scaling would prevent new cemental deposition or reattachment of periodontal fibers. Thus, all efforts for removal of subgingival calculus are essential to provide for an ideal healing environment.

The root surfaces within a periodontal pocket are exposed to plaque organisms and a variety of biologically active substances. The cemental surfaces may undergo decalcification and resorptive changes to a depth of as much as 300 μm. Endotoxins produced by Gram-negative bacteria are absorbed into the cementum. An inhibitory action of this absorbed endotoxin on fibroblast proliferation in tissue culture has been demonstrated. Therefore, reattachment to cementum by the connective tissue of a pocket may require root planing to a depth in the cementum, which would remove all the absorbed endotoxin.

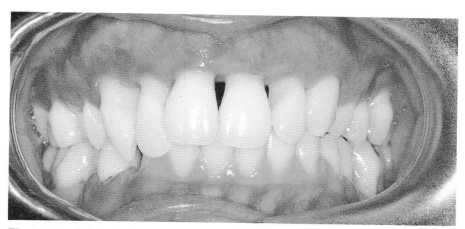

Fig. 1-23 Clinical photographs of patient in Fig. 1-22 at age 28. Note relative absence of gingival inflammation in spite of severe bone loss and pocket depth.

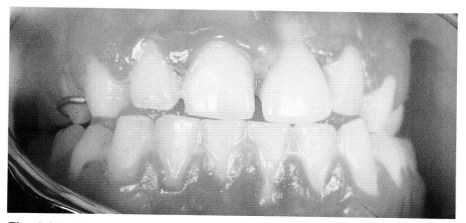

Fig. 1-24 Acute necrotizing ulcerative gingivitis in a young adult. Note necrosis and flattening of the interdental papillae.

Types of periodontal disease

Periodontal disease consists of a broad spectrum of diseases that have different incidence rates, age of onset, distribution in the dentition, and microbial etiology.

Gingivitis

Gingivitis is the most prevalent and mildest manifestation of periodontal disease. It is associated with bacterial plaque. The lesion, by definition, is limited to inflammation of the marginal gingiva with no loss of attachment of periodontal tissues. Increased sulcus depth is caused only by the gingival enlargement and is reversible to normal levels by removal of the bacterial plaque and calculus. Onset may

Variation in Health and Disease

Figs. 1-25a and b   Subacute necrotizing ulcerative gingivitis of long standing.

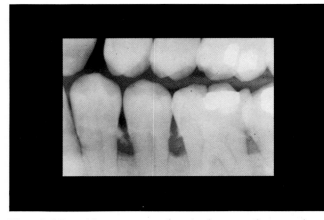

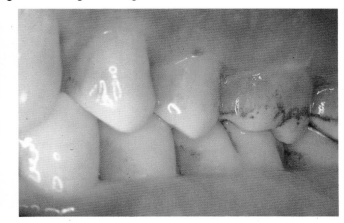

Fig. 1-25a   Note spurs of calculus on the proximal surfaces. Bone loss is limited to only the proximal surface, with facial and lingual bone intact.

Fig. 1-25b   Loss of interdental papillae, with craters and the absence of acute gingival inflammation.

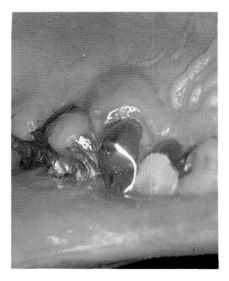

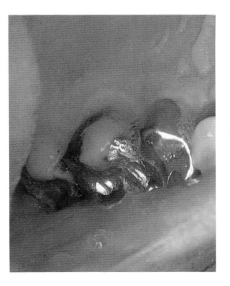

Fig. 1-26a Acute periodontal abscess palatal to teeth 3 and 4.

Fig. 1-26b Healing after deep scaling.

be extremely early, with a peak in severity occurring during puberty. Marginal inflammation can be initiated at any age by poor oral hygiene practices. The lesion frequently progresses to the deeper structures but can remain stable for many years.

Adult periodontitis

Adult periodontitis occurs with a very high frequency and is characterized by extension of the inflammation apically with detachment of periodontal ligament fibers, loss of alveolar bone, and pocket for-

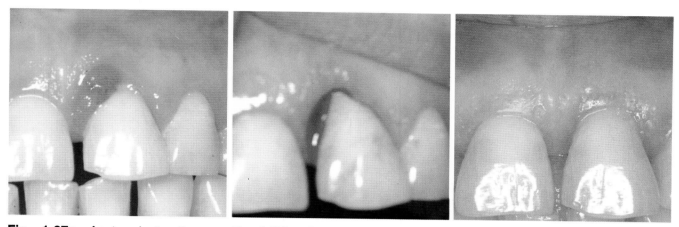

Fig. 1-27a Acute destructive granulation lesion. Note how granulation tissue has forced the original gingival margin away from the tooth.

Fig. 1-27b Surgical excision is the treatment usually required.

Fig. 1-27c Healing in 1 month.

mation. Gingival inflammation of various degrees of intensity is associated with the periodontal lesion. The disease is also associated with plaque and involves such local factors as overhanging restorations, which enhance the onset and progress of the lesion by increasing plaque retention. The lesions appear most frequently in the molars, though no specific patterns of disease are discernable. The lesion progresses at variable rates when untreated, undergoing periods of activity, remission, and even spontaneous healing. Progress of the lesion is usually accompanied by an increase in bleeding on gentle probing, indicating the presence of deep sulcular epithelial ulceration and vascular change. The variations in clinical appearance, the rate of progress, and its responses to treatment suggest that adult periodontitis represents more than one disease.

Other periodontal diseases

The remaining periodontal diseases occur with considerably less frequency and include juvenile periodontitis (periodontosis), postjuvenile periodontitis and forms of necrotizing gingivitis.

Juvenile periodontitis

Juvenile periodontitis (periodontosis), a relatively rare disease, begins around the age of puberty. The most frequent distribution of periodontal destruction in juvenile periodontitis is a bilaterally symmetric semilunar bone loss about the incisors and first molars (Figs. 1-21a and b). Other patterns of destruction are occasionally found: bone loss primarily in the premolars and second molars and a broadly disseminated type, where most teeth are affected. Tooth mobility and pathologic migration are also frequent findings.

The onset of juvenile periodontitis is rapid, with severe pocket development in the absence of commensurate quantities of bacterial plaque, calculus, or visible gingival inflammation. It is believed that a specific organism, *Actinobacillus actinomycetem-comitans,* is the primary pathogen, with resultant production of serum antibodies to subspecies in most diseased individuals. The organism is believed to invade the gingival tissues, which has implications in the choice of treatment methods. The presence of near-perfect bilateral symmetry of the periodontal destruction in the localized forms suggests the possibility of tooth-borne systemic predisposing factors, which are little understood. Defects in leukocyte function, as well as a strong hereditary predisposition, are also present in most cases.

The majority of patients exhibit broader areas of periodontal destruction as they age, and a concomitant increase in local etiologic agents and inflammation (Fig. 1-22).

Necrotizing gingivitis

Acute necrotizing ulcerative gingivitis has a unique pathogenesis. The disease is manifest initially as necrosis of the gingiva, which begins at the apex of the pyramidal interdental papilla (Figs. 1-23 and 1-24). Ulcerated craters with some overlying necrotic tissue are produced. The tips of the papillae may only be blunted, but, in some instances, the necrosis can extend to the crestal bone. Clinically, only a curtain of inflamed gingival tissue remains on the facial and lingual sides of the interdental embrasure. An instrument placed proximally can be moved mesiodistally from one tooth to the other without encountering any gingival tissue. The gingiva is acutely inflamed and very tender. The patient may exhibit a low-grade fever and general malaise. The etiology is in part related to invasion of the tissues by spirochetes prodromally. Other organisms gain entry through the ulcerated proximal gingiva. The disease has a strongly psychosomatic component, with anxiety and depressed states frequently preceding the onset of disease. Individuals who are subject to such psychologic states may have recurrent bouts of infection with long periods of remission. The plaque bacteria that colonize the unhealed craters undergo calcification so that heavy accumulations of spurlike calculus are frequently found (Figs. 1-25a and b). Diagnostically, the presence of such calculus spurs associated with bone loss only on proximal surfaces is almost pathognomonic of recurrent ulcerative gingivitis. Success in treatment depends in part on control of the psychologic component of the cause. Should this control be impossible, total eradication of the disease may be very difficult.

Periodontal abscess and granulation lesions. Two acute variations of postjuvenile and adult periodontitis are worthy of special attention: periodontal abscess and granulation tissue-induced rapid bone loss. Periodontal abscess is an acute form of disease, usually occurring within an existing periodontal pocket. Though the etiology is obscure, it is assumed that alone or in combination, either reduction of local resistance or variation in bacterial flora toward actively infective organisms is the cause. Usually, all the signs of abscess are present:

inflammation, swelling, pain, and final localization and pointing of the abscess with rupture and release of pus (Fig. 1-26a). Early intervention by drainage and root cleansing subgingivally, either as a flap or closed procedure, usually terminates the process (Fig. 1-26b). Frequently, the rapid bone loss associated with the abscess will regenerate.

Rapid-onset granulation tissue bone destruction is a less frequently encountered pathologic condition. In this condition, teeth with normal periodontiums or shallow pockets can have portions of the attachment apparatus undergo rapid destruction resulting from the formation of highly vascular granulation tissue. The actively proliferating granulation tissue forces the gingiva away from the teeth, destroys underlying bone, and forms deep pockets in a matter of days. A line of demarcation is evident between the newly formed granulation tissue and the gingiva (Fig. 1-27a). The lesion has been associated with subgingival overgrowths of *Bacteroides capillosus*. To effectively eliminate the lesion, one must surgically excise all the granulation tissue. Bone regrowth is common, although recurrence of the lesion is not unusual (Figs. 1-27b and c).

References

Adelson, L.J., et al. In vitro cytotoxicity of periodontally diseased root surfaces. J. Periodontol. 51:700, 1980.

Ainamo, J., et al. Anatomical characteristics of gingiva. A clinical and microscopic study of the free and attached gingiva. J. Periodontol. 37:5, 1966.

Aleo, J.J., et al. The presence and biologic activity of cementum-bound endotoxin. J. Periodontol. 45:672, 1974.

Anerud, K.E., et al. Periodontal disease in three young adult populations. J. Periodont. Res. 18:655, 1983.

Attstrom, R., et al. Complement factors in gingival crevice material from healthy and inflamed gingiva in humans. J. Periodont. Res. 10:19, 1975.

Brown, L.R., et al. Effect of radiation induced xerostosmia on human oral microflora. J. Dent. Res. 54:740, 1975.

Ciancio, S.C., et al. The principal fibers of the periodontal ligament. Periodontics 5:76, 1967.

Cianciola, L.J., et al. Defective polymorphonuclear leukocyte function in human periodontal disease. Nature 265:445, 1977.

Cohen, D.W., et al. A longitudinal investigation of the periodontal changes during pregnancy and fifteen months postpartum. Part II. J. Periodontol. 42:653, 1971.

Cohen, D.W., et al. Diabetes mellitus and periodontal disease: Two-year longitudinal observations. J. Periodontol. 41:709, 1970.

Cooper, P.G., et al. Cell populations associated with gingival bleeding. J. Periodontol. 54:497, 1983.

Courtois, G. J., et al. Acute necrotizing ulcerative gingivitis. A transmission electron microscope study. J. Periodontol. 54:671, 1983.

Davenport, R.H., et al. Histometric comparison of active and inactive lesions of advanced periodontitis. J. Periodontol. 53:285, 1982.

Donnenfeld, O.W., et al. A nine-month clinical and histological study of patients on diphenylhydantoin following gingivectomy. J. Periodontol. 45:547, 1974.

Engelberger, T., et al. Correlation among papilla bleeding index, other clinical indices and histologically determined inflammation of gingival papilla. J. Clin. Periodontol. 10:579, 1983.

Fine, D.H., et al. Preliminary characterization of material eluted from the roots of periodontally diseased teeth. J. Periodont. Res. 15:10, 1980.

36

Variation in Health and Disease

Gavin, J.B., et al. Ultrastructural feature of chronic marginal gingivitis. J. Periodont. Res. 5:19, 1970.

Gher, M.W., et al. Linear variation of root surface area of the maxillary first molar. J. Periodontol. 56:39, 1985.

Giddon, D.B., et al. Prevalence of reported cases of acute necrotizing ulcerative gingivitis in a university population. J. Periodontol. 34:366, 1963.

Glickman, I., et al. Chronic desquaimative gingivitis—its nature and treatment. J. Periodontol. 35:397, 1964.

Goldman, H.M., et al. The topography and role of the gingival fibers. J. Dent. Res. 30:331, 1951.

Goodson, J.M., et al. Prostaglandin E2 levels and human periodontal disease. Prostaglandins 6:81, 1974.

Gorlin, R.J., et al. Genetics and periodontal disease. J. Periodontol. 38:5, 1967.

Hancock, E.B., et al. The relationship between gingival crevicular fluid and gingival inflammation—a clinical and histologic study. J. Periodontol. 50:13, 1979.

Hatfield, C.A., et al. Cytotoxic effects of periodontally involved surfaces of human teeth. Arch. Oral Biol. 16:465, 1971.

Hellden, L., et al. Enhanced emigration of crevicular leukocytes mediated by factors in human dental plaque. Scand. J. Dent. Res. 81:123, 1973.

Holm-Pederson, P., et al. Experimental gingivitis in young and elderly individuals. J. Clin. Periodont. 2:14, 1975.

Hormond, J., et al. Juvenile periodontitis. Localization of bone loss in relation to sex, age and teeth. J. Clin. Periodont. 6:707, 1979.

Horton, J.E., et al. Human lymphoproliferative reaction to saliva and dental plaque deposits. An in-vitro correlation with periodontal disease. J. Periodontol. 43:522, 1972.

Ivanyi, L., et al. Cell mediated immunity in human periodontal disease. Cytotoxicity, migration inhibition and lymphocyte transformation studies. Immunology 22:141, 1972.

Jorgensen, R.J., et al. Variations in inheritance and expression of gingival fibromatosis. J. Periodontol. 45:472, 1974.

Kapur, R.N., et al. Diphenylhydantoin induced gingival hyperplasia. Its relationship to dose and serum level. Develop. Med. Child. Neurol. 15:483, 1973.

Kennedy, J.E., et al. Effect of inflammation on collateral circulation of the gingiva. J. Periodont. Res. 9:147, 1974.

Kornman, K.S., et al. Physiological and ultrastructural characterization of a new bacteriodes species (Bacteroides capillus) isolated from severe localized periodontitis. J. Periodont. Res. 16:542, 1981.

Larato, D.C., et al. Alveolar plate fenestrations and dehiscences of the human skull. Oral. Surg. 29:816, 1970.

Lehner, T., et. al. Immunological aspects of juvenile periodontitis (periodontosis). J. Periodont. Res. 9:261, 1974.

Lindhe, J., et al. Some microbiological and histopathological features of periodontal disease in man. J. Periodontol. 51:264, 1980.

Listgarten, M.A., et al. Structure of the microbial flora associated with periodontal health and disease in man. A light and electron microscopic study. J. Periodontol. 47:1, 1976.

Loe, H., et al. Experimental gingivitis in man. J. Periodontol. 36:177, 1965.

Lopez, N.J., et al. Inflammatory effects of periodontally diseased cementum studied by autogenous dental root implants in man. J. Periodontol. 51:505, 1980.

Mackler, B.F., et al. Immunoglobulin bearing lymphocytes and plasma cells in human periodontal disease. J. Periodont. Res. 12:37, 1977.

Mackler, B.F., et al. Ig G subclasses in human periodontal disease. II. Cytophilic and membrane Ig G subclass immunoglobulin. J. Periodont. Res. 13:433, 1978.

Manson, J.D., et al. Clinical features of juvenile periodontitis (periodontosis). J. Periodontol. 45:636, 1974.

Melcher, A.H., et al. The connective tissue of the periodontium. In Melcher, A.H., and Brown, W.H. (eds.) Biology of the Periodontium. New York: Academic Press, Inc., 1969.

Mendieta, C.F., et al. Biosynthesis of prostaglandins in gingiva of patients with chronic periodontitis. J. Periodontol. 56:44, 1985.

Moskow, B.S. Spontaneous arrest of advanced periodontal disease without treatment. J. Periodontol. 49:465, 1978.

Moulton, R., et al. Emotional factors in periodontal disease. Oral Surg. 5:933, 1952.

Murphy, P.J., et al. An altered gingival attachment epithelium: A result of the enzyme hyaluronidase. Periodontics 6:105, 1968.

Murray P.A., et al. Gingival crevice neutrophil function in periodontal lesions. J. Periodont. Res. 15:463, 1980.

Newman, H.N., et al. Update in plaque and periodontal disease. J. Clin. Periodont. 7:251, 1980.

Newman, M.A., et al. Predominant cultivable microbiota in periodontosis. J. Periodont. Res. 12:120, 1977.

Nielsen, I.M., et al. Interproximal periodontal intrabony defects. Prevalence, localization and etiologic factors. J. Clin. Periodont. 7:187, 1980.

Nisengard, R.J., et al. The role of immunology in periodontal disease. J. Periodontol. 48:505, 1977.

Oliver R.C., et al. The correlation between clinical scoring, exudate measurement and microscopic evaluation of inflammation of the gingiva. J. Periodontol. 40:210, 1969.

Orban, B., et al. Oral Histology and Embryology. 3rd ed. St. Louis: The C.V. Mosby Co., 1953.

Page, R.C., et al. Collagen fiber bundles of the normal gingiva. Arch. Oral Biol. 19:1039, 1974.

Page, R.C., et al. Pathogenesis of inflammatory periodontal disease. A summary of current work. Lab. Invest. 33:235, 1976.

Payne, W.A., et al. Histopathologic features of the initial and early stages of experimental gingivitis in man. J. Periodont. Res. 10:51, 1975.

Patters, M.R., et al. Blastogenic response of human lymphocytes to oral bacterial antigens: Comparison of individuals with periodontal disease to normal and edentulous subjects. Infect. Immun. 14:1213, 1976.

Pennel, B.M., et al. Predisposing factors in the etiology of chronic inflammatory periodontal disease. J. Periodontol. 48:517, 1977.

Ranney, R.R., et al. Relationship between attachment loss and precipitating serum antibodies to Actinobacillus Actinomycetemcomitans in adolescent and young adults having severe periodontal destruction. J. Periodontol. 53:1, 1982.

Rizzo, A.A., et al. The possible role of hydrogen sulfide in human periodontal disease. I. Hydrogen sulfide production in periodontal pockets. Periodontics 5:233, 1967.

Saglie, F.R., et al. Identification of tissue invading bacteria in human periodontal disease. J. Periodont. Res. 17:452, 1982.

Sandholm, L., et al. Concentration of serum protease inhibitors and immunoglobulins in juvenile periodontitis. J. Periodont. Res. 18:527, 1983.

Schenkein, H., et al. Gingival fluid and serum in periodontal disease. II. Evidence for activation of complement components C3, C3 proactivation and C4 in gingival fluid. J. Periodontol. 48:778, 1977.

Selvig, R.A., et al. Ultrastructural changes in cementium and adjacent connective tissue in periodontal disease. Acta Odontol. Scand. 24:459, 1966.

Selvig, R.A., et al. Attachment of plaque and calculus to tooth surfaces. J. Periodont. Res. 5:8, 1970.

Seymour, G.J., et al. Conversion of a stable T-cell lesion to a progressive B-cell lesion in the pathogenesis of chronic inflammatory periodontal disease. An hypothesis. J. Clin. Periodontol. 6:267, 1979.

Shapiro, L., et al. Sulcular exudate flow in gingival inflammation. J. Periodontol. 50:301, 1979.

Shilletoe, E.J., et al. Immunoglobulin and complement in crevicular fluid, serum and saliva in man. Arch. Oral Biol. 17:341, 1972.

Slots, J., et al. Subgingival microflora and periodontal disease. J. Clin. Periodontol. 6:351, 1979.

Slots, J., et al. The predominant cultivable microflora of advanced periodontitis. Scand. J. Dent. Res. 85:114, 1977.

Spektor, M.D., et al. Clinical studies of one family manifesting rapidly progressive juvenile and prepubertal periodontitis. J. Periodontol. 56:93, 1985.

Suomi, J.E., et al. Patterns of gingivitis. J. Periodontol. 39:71, 1969.

Solis-Goffar, M.C., et al. Hydrogen sulfide production from gingival crevicular fluid. J. Periodontol. 51:603, 1980.

Stashenko, P., et al. T cell responses of periodontal disease patients and healthy subjects to oral microorganisms. J. Periodont. Res. 18:587, 1983.

Tanner, A.C.R., et al. A study of the bacteria associated with advancing periodontitis in man. J. Clin. Periodont. 6:278, 1979.

Thilander, H., et al. Epithelial changes in gingivitis. J. Periodont. Res. 3:303, 1968.

Van Dyke, T.E., et al. Periodontal disease and impaired neutrophile functions. J. Periodont. Res. 17:492, 1982.

van Palenstein-Helderman, W.H., et al. Bacterial viable counts in crevices of non-inflamed and inflamed gingiva. J. Periodont. Res. 11:25, 1976.

Wohl, L.M., et al. Collagenase production by lymphokine-activated macrophages. Science 187:261, 1975.

Zachrisson, B., et al. A comparative histological study of clinically normal and chronically inflamed gingiva from the same individuals. Odontol. Foren. Tidskr. 76:179, 1968.

Zander, H.A., et al. The attachment of calculus to root surfaces. J. Periodontol. 27:16, 1953.

Chapter 2

Objectives of Definitive Deep Scaling

The relationship of calculus and other accretions to disease was understood in ancient times. In the 11th century, Albucasus in the text *The Sayings of Pythagoros on Scaling the Teeth with Iron Instruments* described the rationale for treatment of gum disease as well as instruments and techniques required. The technical difficulties inherent in the removal of all calcareous deposits were recognized, and repeated scalings of a given area were suggested. Rather heroic scaling and soft tissue curettage were suggested and practiced by Riggs in the late 19th century.

In the early 1900s, Hutchinson's technique included "closed" deep scaling as well as "open" root curettage after making a vertical incision in the gingiva to expose the root surfaces. In all instances, removal of subgingival deposit and the incidental elimination of all subgingival plaque were the objectives. Smoothed root surfaces were the endpoint of these objectives and subsequently described deep scaling procedures. The removal of subgingival deposit and the disruption of subgingival plaque would in the majority of cases significantly reduce gingival inflammation and pocket depth. The results so obtained were much superior to treatment methods that depended on topical or systemic medications alone. Refinements in hand instrument design helped simplify the deep scaling procedure, making it the cornerstone of periodontal therapy.

Ideally, the goal of all periodontal therapy is to reconstitute the periodontal tissues in their original form and relationships. Such a result occurs consistently only when the disease is completely reversible, as in early marginal gingivitis, when no connective tissue attachment of the periodontium to the root has been lost. Once a true periodontal pocket depth has developed, reconstitution of the periodontium is only rarely obtainable by deep scaling alone. Thus, the objective of deep scaling in treatment of periodontitis is to eliminate or reduce the size of plaque retentive periodontal pockets by either tissue shrinkage or "reattachment" to the tooth surface.

When deep scaling is used as the sole means of treatment for a given periodontal pocket, the procedure must be extremely thorough. The technique is known as *definitive deep scaling*.

If the aim of scaling is to reduce gingival inflammation in preparation for surgical procedures in deeper pockets, the requirements are less stringent, since good tissue tone can result from less than perfect deep scaling. This procedure is presurgical scaling.

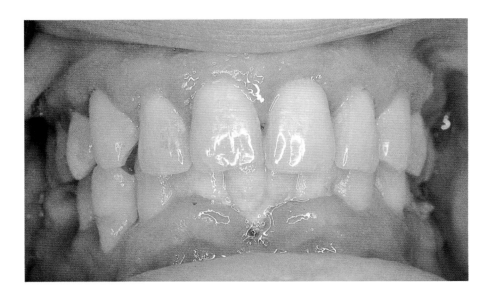

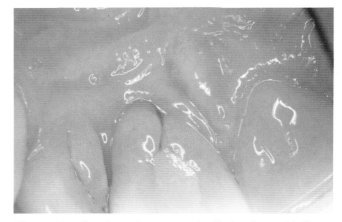

Fig. 2-1 Advanced periodontitis case exhibiting inflammatory gingival hyperplasia directly associated with heavy bacterial plaque and calculus. Teeth 9, 10, and 11 were very lightly scaled 1 week before the photograph was taken, with reduction of gingival inflammation compared with teeth 6, 7, and 8. These cases response best to definitive deep scaling.

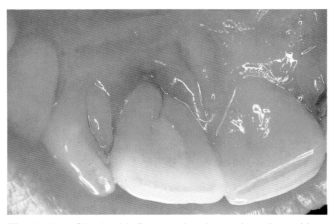

Fig. 2-2a Gingival inflammation in conjunction with a deep pocket along the developmental groove on the palatal surface of tooth 8. Supragingival plaque was light, but subgingival calculus and plaque were moderately heavy.

Fig. 2-2b Pocket closure and elimination of inflammation after deep scaling.

Variations in gingival tissue reaction to local plaque and calculus

Though the pathologic processes leading to pocket formation would appear to be identical, variations in soft tissue responses in individuals with similar severity of periodontitis can range between slight to very severe gingivitis. When the pathologic potential of the subgingival deposits, both hard and soft, is manifested by an exuberant inflammatory enlargement of the gingiva with spontaneous or copious bleeding during instrumentation, the most dramatic responses will attend deep scaling and root planing (Fig. 2-1). Gingival inflammation will subside, reducing gingival enlargement. In addition, a

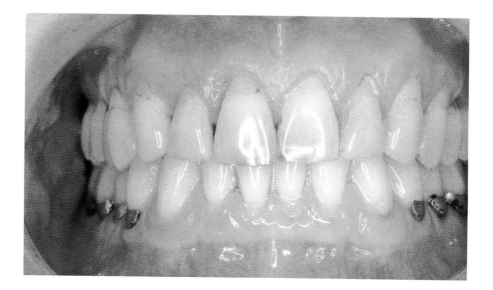

Fig. 2-3 Deep pocket on distal surface of tooth 8 has inflammation masked by thick gingiva so that clinically one might not suspect the presence of a pocket.

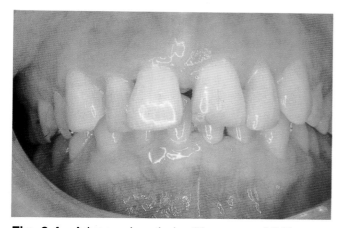

Fig. 2-4 Advanced periodontitis case exhibiting cyanotic gingival response with little change in gingival size and contour.

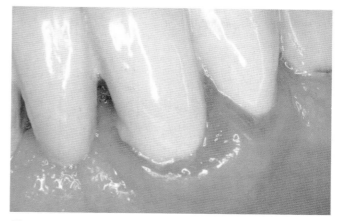

Fig. 2-5 Proliferative inflammatory gingival response.

gain in attachment level measurement is frequently encountered, resulting in reduced clinical pocket depths.

The clinical changes are reflected in the histologic changes, which include reconstitution of the fibrous connective tissues of the gingiva, as well as the circumferential fibers. Thus, the gingiva hugs the tooth surface tightly and cannot be readily retracted. Apart from tissue shrinkage, measurable pocket depth reductions can result in two ways. First, the resistance to periodontal probe penetration at the base of the pocket may be increased when the gingival connective tissue attachment is normal compared with the inflamed state. Second, a long epithelial attachment to the root surface, resistant to gentle probing, frequently develops (Figs. 2-2a and b).

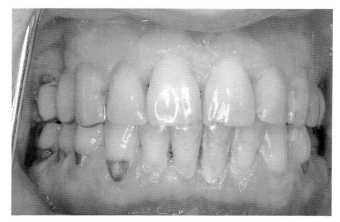

Fig. 2-6a Clinically noninflammatory gingival response.

Fig. 2-6b Radiograph showing extensive disease of case in Fig. 2-6a.

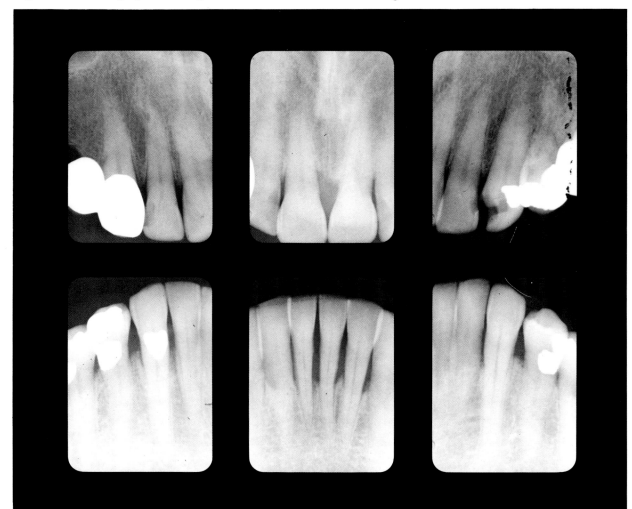

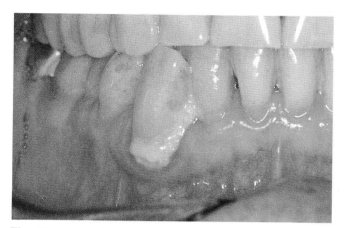

Fig. 2-7 Local gingival inflammation associated with plaque and calculus.

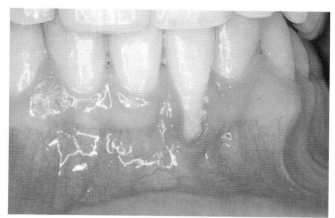

Fig. 2-8 Localized gingival recession resulting from a combination of thin gingiva and alveolar process because of tooth prominence and gingival inflammation.

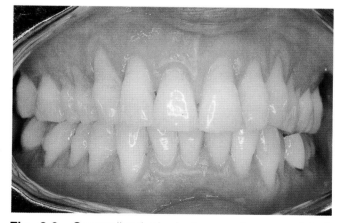

Fig. 2-9 Generalized gingival recession associated with a periodontitis of oversized teeth in thin alveolar processes. Moderate plaque and subgingival calculus produce moderate gingivitis.

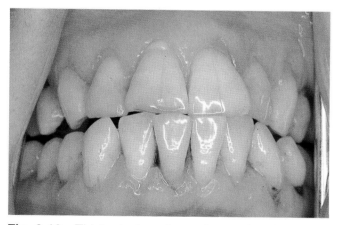

Fig. 2-10 Thick gingiva of an advanced periodontitis appear more normal than they are because of masking of the underlying pathologic condition. Slight bleeding is evident after probing pockets.

When the gingiva exhibits little clinical inflammation, because of thick gingival tissue which masks gingival inflammatory changes immediately adjacent to the subgingival plaque, only minor pocket depth changes may result from deep scaling (Fig. 2-3). Under these circumstances, gingival bleeding after instrumentation will cease, but gingival height will be relatively unchanged due to the bulk of uninflamed gingiva. Changes in the color and texture of the gingiva are minimal. Similarly, pockets in periodontitis cases with gingiva (which exhibits no inflammatory enlargement and exhibits color changes of a cyanotic nature) are only minimally improved by deep scaling (Fig. 2-4).

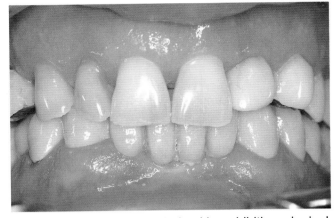

Fig. 2-11 Advanced periodontitis exhibiting gingival cyanosis with no gingival enlargement of relatively thin gingiva.

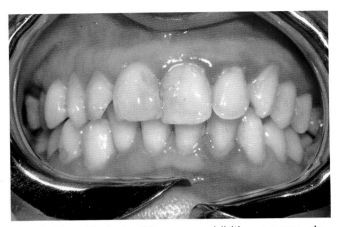

Fig. 2-12a Periodontitis case exhibiting severe gingival inflammation.

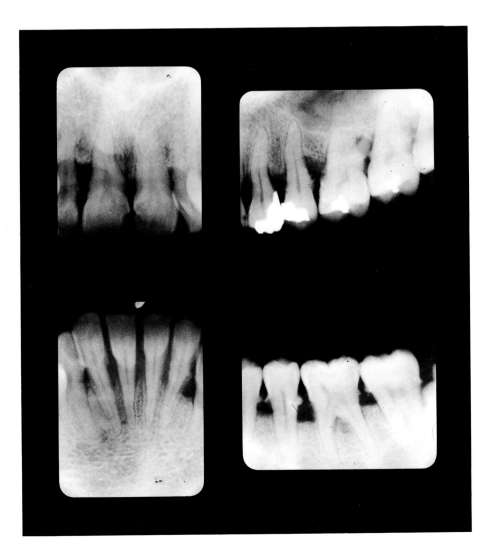

Fig. 2-12b Heavy spurs of calculus with horizontal bone loss in periodontitis.

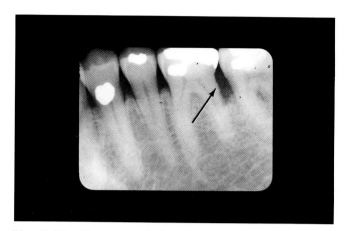

Fig. 2-13 Severe periodontal breakdown associated with light subgingival platelike and slightly nodular calculus and little inflammation, which suggests a poor response to definitive deep scaling.

Thus, variations in the gingival tissue reaction to local plaque and calculus coupled with other tissue changes are important factors in developing a rational role for deep scaling within a treatment plan. A few of the multitude of pathologic variations in the gingiva and the periodontium may include:

1. Proliferative inflammation (Fig. 2-5).
2. Clinically little or no inflamed tissue (Figs. 2-6a and b).
3. Plaque-induced localized inflammation on prominent nonbrushed surface (Fig. 2-7).
4. Localized recession related to root position and plaque-induced inflammation (Fig. 2-8).
5. General recession with moderate inflammation (Fig. 2-9).
6. Gingival inflammation, response masked by thick gingiva. Note suppuration labial to maxillary right central incisor (Fig. 2-10).
7. Cyanotic response with no bleeding on gentle probing in thin gingiva (Fig. 2-11).

Such gingival and periodontal pathologic responses should be correlated with the presence of obvious local causative factors as well as the form and quantity of subgingival calculus and bacterial plaque.

Aids in predicting clinical changes from deep scaling

The factors that aid in predicting the clinical changes resulting from deep scaling are the degree of inflammatory tissue enlargement, the ease of bleeding on instrumentation, the relative proportion and dis-

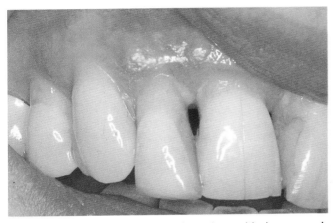

Fig. 2-14 Deep periodontal pocket with heavy calculus but with very slight overlying gingival inflammation. Note considerable suppuration when gingiva is pressed. Pocket closure by definitive deep scaling does not usually occur.

tribution of inflammation in the gingival wall (tissue thickness), and the correlation of pathologic change with eradicable local etiology. Thus, for example, the greater the amount of subgingival plaque and spurlike calculus associated with severe gingival inflammation and pocket formation, the better the response of the gingiva to deep scaling (Figs. 2-12a and b).

The gingiva, overlying deep periodontal pockets that are scaled, should assume normal color and surface characteristics. Even without pocket closure, suppuration from the pocket should cease. Ideally, such gingival tissue should have an intact sulcular epithelium and a minimal area of altered connective tissue adjacent to the deepest part of the sulcular epithelium.

Subgingival calculus

Subgingival calculus has been described as varying from a thin, platelike deposit covering most of the pocket cementum to heavy, spurred formations on portions of the root surface. One must be cognizant of these morphologic variations since they are related to tissue reaction and response to treatment. For example, there are a small number of cases of periodontitis with minimal amounts of thin, platelike calculus exhibiting severe pocket depth and bone loss but with little or no gingival inflammation (Fig. 2-13). Removal of these small amounts of calculus and subgingival plaque, as might be expected, produce no marked periodontal benefits. Awareness of the rate of subgingival calculus development is important since there is a distinct relationship between the rapidity of subgingival calculus reformation and the long-term prognosis of periodontal cases.

Suppuration

Suppuration from the gingival sulcus is the clinical manifestation of leukocyte chemotaxis by sulcular organisms. Though an increase in the amount of pus occurs with actively progressive disease, there does not seem to be a quantitative relationship to disease activity. Applying gentle pressure to the gingival wall of an untreated pocket will most frequently express some pus. The conclusion that such a pocket is undergoing active extension, however, may be unwarranted since some patients observed over many years have unaltered deep pockets that are actively suppurating. This observation is in consort with the fact that leukocyte transmigration of the epithelium is a characteristic of the gingival response to bacterial plaque. Factors that limit passage of the pus, such as close adaptation of the gingival pocket wall to the tooth as opposed to easily retracted gingiva, may account for differences in expressable exudate volume (Fig. 2-14). Retracted gingiva frequently allows heavy subgingival plaque buildup, which when expressed by pressure, may suggest an erroneously large volume of pus present, when in fact the bacterial plaque accounts for much of the volume. Visible suppuration must therefore be considered as a sign of a lack of health rather than as a certain indicator as of actively progressing disease.

The odoriferous substances resulting from oral bacterial metabolism include hydrogen sulfide, indoles, and pyrimidines. These substances are related to increased accumulations of plaque and subsequent gingivitis. Differences in odor of subgingival exudate can vary enormously. Occasionally, a distinctive acrid odor is associated with moderate to severe suppuration, moderate gingival inflammation, and heavy subgingival calculus. Though research correlating odors and bacterial constituents of subgingival plaque is almost nonexistent, such information could provide an additional parameter to our diagnostic armamentarium for further definition of the disease process. Oral odor is frequently the result of subgingival bacterial metabolism and is therefore eliminated subsequent to reduction of pocket depth. In cases of acute necrotizing gingivitis, the combination of gingival necrosis and bacterial organisms produce a characteristic odor. The almost pathognomonic odor, as one would expect, disappears as the acute phase subsides.

Since the response to root scaling can fall within a range of responses, one must decide what role deep scaling will play in the total therapy of a given periodontal case. Guidelines based on clinical experience are helpful in making such a decision. Such clinical experience presupposes highly effective technical skill and broad application of the technique.

References

Cantor, M.T., et al. The effect of various interdental stimulators on the keratinization of the interdental col. Periodontics 3:243, 1965.

Garrett, J.S., et al. Effects of non-surgical periodontal therapy in humans. J. Clin. Periodontol. 10:545, 1983.

Helden, L.B., et al. The effect of tetracycline and/or scaling on human periodontal disease. J. Clin. Periodontol. 6:22, 1979.

Hinrichs, J.E., et al. Effects of scaling and root planing on subgingival microbial proportions standardized in terms of their naturally occurring distribution. J. Periodontol. 56:187, 1985.

Jones, W.A., et al. The effectiveness of in vivo root planing in removing endotoxin from the roots of periodontally involved teeth. J. Periodontol. 49:377, 1978.

Kantor, M., et al. The behavior of angular bony defects following reduction of inflammation. J. Periodontol. 51:705, 1980.

Khatiblou, F.A., et al. Root surface smoothness or roughness in periodontal treatment—a clinical study. J. Periodontol. 54:365, 1983.

Lindhe, J., et al. Scaling and root planing shallow pockets. J. Clin. Periodontol. 9:415, 1982.

Listgarten, M.A., et al. Relative distribution of bacteria at clinically healthy and periodontally diseased sites in humans. J. Clin. Periodontol. 5:115, 1978.

Listgarten, M.A., et al. The effect of tetracycline and/or scaling on human periodontal disease. Clinical, microbiological and histological observations. J. Clin. Periodontol. 5:246, 1978.

Moskow, B.S., et al. The response of the gingival sulci to instrumentation, a histologic investigation. The scaling procedure. J. Periodontol. 33:282, 1962.

Moskow, B.S., et al. The response of gingival sulci to instrumentation, a histologic investigation. II. Gingival curettage. J. Periodontol. 35:113, 1964.

Osterberg, S., et al. Long term effects of tetracycline on subgingival microflora. J. Clin. Periodontol. 6:133, 1979.

Ramfjord, S., et al. The gingival sulcus and the periodontal pocket immediately following scaling of the teeth. J. Periodontol. 25:167, 1954.

Selvig, K.A., et al. Periodontally diseased cementum studied by correlated microradiography, electron probe and electron microscopy. J. Periodont. Res. 12:419, 1977.

Chapter 3

Predictable Results from Definitive Deep Scaling

Case types amenable to deep scaling

Good responses are dependent on case type and tissue reaction.

Marginal gingivitis

Marginal gingivitis in which the cause is clearly local plaque and calculus is amenable to deep scaling (Figs. 3-1a and b). A distinct relationship should be readily demonstrated between areas of inflammation and local plaque accumulation and calculus deposition. The areas most frequently inflamed are the buccal surface of maxillary molars, the facial surface of some anterior teeth, and the lingual surface of mandibular anterior teeth and molars. Since the essential etiologic agent is bacterial plaque, effective oral hygiene procedures are presupposed in all successful therapy.

Inflammation limited to the palatal gingiva of the maxillary anterior teeth or the labial gingiva of the mandibular anterior teeth and adja-

Fig. 3-1a Marginal gingivitis about maxillary central incisors before definitive deep scaling.

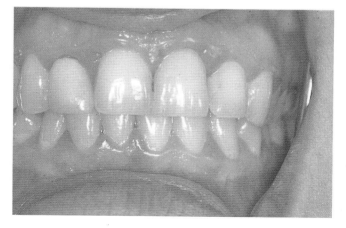

Fig. 3-1b After definitive deep scaling. Note complete resolution of inflammatory gingival hyperplasia with resulting gingival shrinkage. Bleeding is the result of vigorous probing.

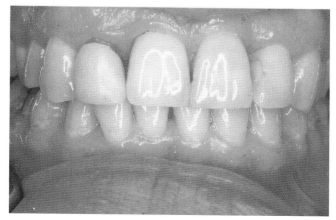

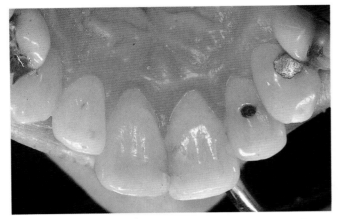

Fig. 3-2a Mouth breathing–induced gingival inflammation palatal to teeth 7, 8, 9, and 10.

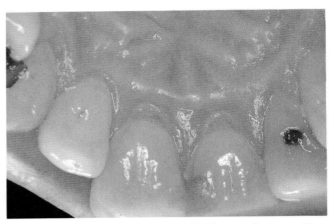

Fig. 3-2b Limited reduction of inflammation resulting from deep scaling. Note prominent band of gingiva 2 to 3 mm from the marginal gingiva. This band of tissue, a mouth-breathing line, is pathognomonic of mouth breathers.

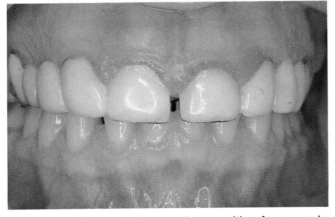

Fig. 3-3a Gingival inflammation resulting from poorly contoured restoration that encroaches on the proximal embrasures.

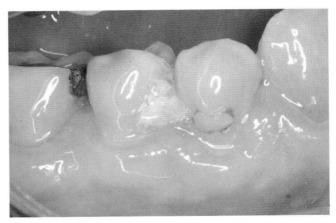

Fig. 3-3b Food impaction as a result of an open contact.

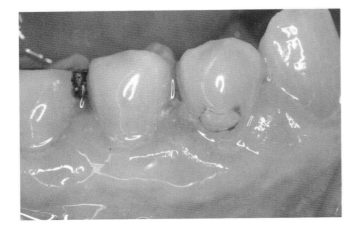

Fig. 3-3c Such food impaction produces gingival inflammation.

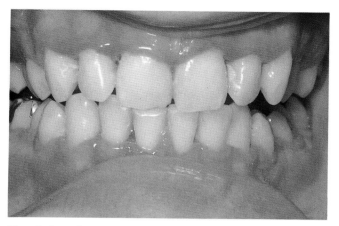

Fig. 3-4a Acute necrotizing gingivitis with interdental craters and inflamed overlying gingiva.

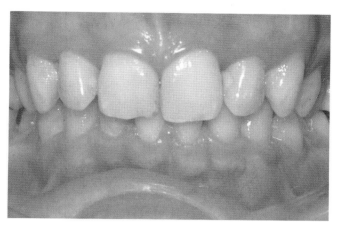

Fig. 3-4b Healing and regrowth of the gingival papillae following debridement and definitive deep scaling.

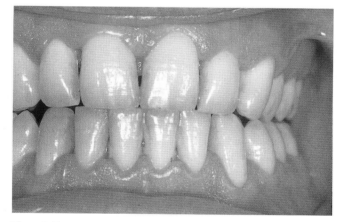

Fig. 3-5a Long-standing recurrent subacute necrotizing gingivitis with generalized 4- to 5-mm interdental gingival craters.

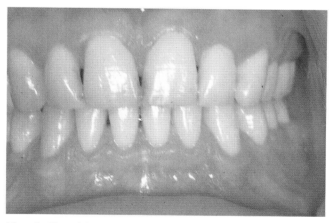

Fig. 3-5b After definitive deep scaling, craters have filled. No pocket depth could be probed, indicating a reattachment during gingival regrowth.

cent to a line of fibrous thickened gingiva should prompt a possible diagnosis of tissue desiccation due to mouth breathing (Figs. 3-2a and b). Inflammation may also be associated with poor restorations and food-retentive areas (Figs. 3-3a to c). In these latter instances, the cause is not eliminated by deep scaling alone, and some inflammation tends to persist until the local cause is eliminated.

Necrotizing ulcerative gingivitis

Necrotizing ulcerative gingivitis in both its acute and moderately advanced subacute forms responds well to deep scaling. In each instance, shallow, interdental, soft tissue craters may be present

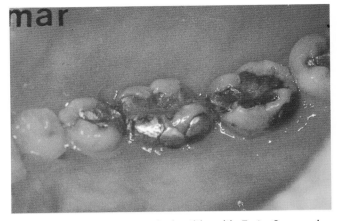

Fig. 3-6a Moderate periodontitis with 5- to 6-mm circumferential pockets exhibiting moderate gingival edema associated with heavy subgingival deposits.

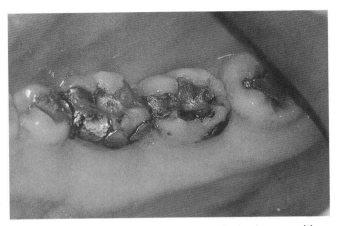

Fig. 3-6b Postscaling shrinkage of gingiva resulting in pocket reductions.

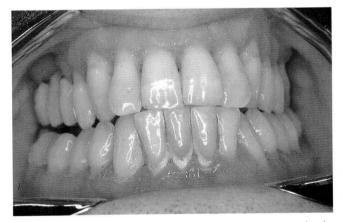

Fig. 3-7a Advanced periodontitis with severe gingival inflammation and bleeding. A combination of deep proximal pockets and furcation involvements were present.

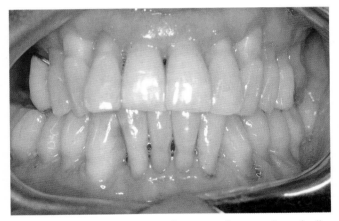

Fig. 3-7b Postdefinitive deep scaling and periodic maintenance for 20 years.

throughout the dentition. In the acute form, subgingival calculus deposits are light, with a combination of necrotic debris and bacterial plaque filling the rapidly formed craters. Gentle debridement of the soft tissue and gentle scaling of the hard tissue wall are all that is required for healing (Figs. 3-4a and b). In the longer-term pathogenesis of the subacute cases, calculus is frequently spurlike and hard to remove. Repeated root planing and debridement of the crater will most frequently induce regrowth of the lost interdental papillae with reattachment of the soft tissue to the tooth (Figs. 3-5a and b).

Moderate periodontitis

Moderate periodontitis (pocket depths to 7mm) characterized by extensive gingival edema can undergo sizable reductions of tissue dimensions after treatment. Pocket depth reductions are dependent on the configuration of the pockets around the teeth. Since pocket reduction is based primarily on tissue shrinkage, circumferential pockets of relatively uniform depths respond most completely (Figs. 3-6a and b). Frequently, shrinkage of the unsupported proximal gingiva causes a slight interproximal saucerlike cratering immediately after treatment. Subsequent changes occur with a slight regrowth of the proximal tissues, and eventually a flat papilla results. However, even initially deep pockets of 8 to 10 mm may often be reduced to managable depths and maintained long term (Figs. 3-7a and b).

As is frequently the case, when pockets are present on proximal surfaces only, shrinkage of the enlarged papillae and edematous marginal gingiva will slightly reduce the proximal pocket. The intact periodontal attachment on the buccal and lingual surfaces of the approximating teeth will prevent the proximal tissue from shrinking completely.

Pocket elimination based on location and configuration

Palatal surface pockets

Palatal pockets that are limited to the palatal surface of anterior teeth or pockets that extend to other surfaces but are markedly deeper on the palatal surface will undergo "closure" after definitive deep scaling. Since palatal tissue is fibrous and rarely undergoes significant tissue shrinkage after scaling, the pocket closure is most likely a reattachment, characterized by a "long epithelial attachment" rather than a new connective tissue attachment. In this location, the reattachment is very stable over long periods of time.

Facial surface pockets

Pockets that are limited to the facial aspect of the root or are significantly deeper on the facial surface respond well to deep scaling. The narrower the pocket, the greater the possibility for success. Since many of these pockets extend apical to the mucogingival line, pocket closure can preclude the necessity of mucogingival surgery.

Proximal deep pockets

Proximal deep pockets on anterior teeth and premolars have a fairly high rate of pocket closure after definitive deep scaling. Deep grooves on proximal surfaces, as are frequently encountered on maxillary first premolars and the lingual surface of maxillary anterior teeth, seem to be a deterrent to successful pocket closure. This deterrence may be the result of difficulties in properly curetting the deeper portions of such vertical grooves.

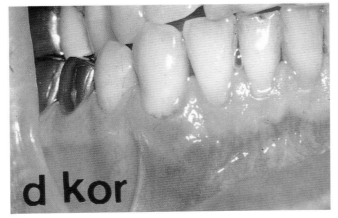

Fig. 3-8a Periodontal abscess on labial side of tooth 27.

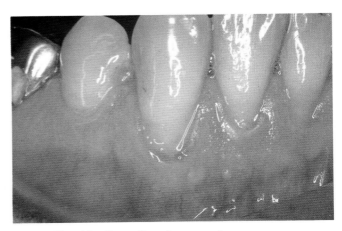

Fig. 3-8b Healing after deep scaling.

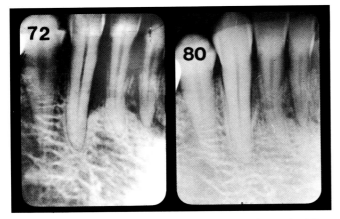

Fig. 3-8c Regrowth of bone with reattachment of the gingiva 8 years after definitive deep scaling.

Abscesses

Acute periodontal abscesses respond well to deep scaling. The responsive nature of acutely inflamed tissues seems to favorably predispose the tissue to regenerate lost attachment and alveolar bone. This reparative ability appears to occur most frequently on single-rooted teeth or on one root of a multirooted tooth (Figs. 3-8a to c). Abscesses related to pockets within the furcations of molars do not respond by regeneration. Occasionally, a pocket that involves the

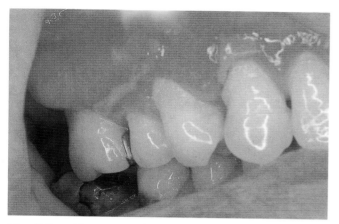

Fig. 3-9a Desquamative gingivitis.

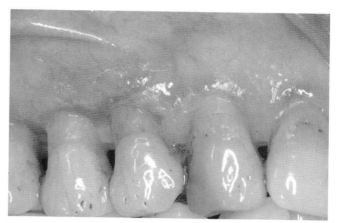

Fig. 3-9b Erosive lichen planus.

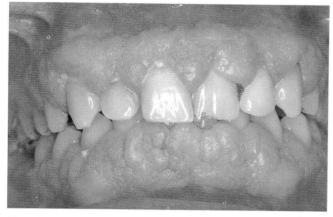

Fig. 3-9c Phenytoin-induced gingival hyperplasia.

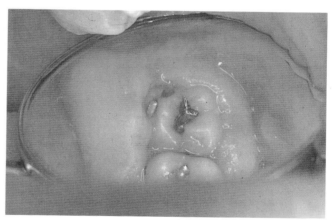

Fig. 3-9d Idiopathic fibromatosis.

furcation of a molar will exhibit deepening on a single root during abscess formation. That portion of the pocket that was rapidly and newly formed will frequently close with deep scaling. However, the bifurcation involvement usually remains unchanged. Those abscessed pockets that can be readily evacuated of pus are most responsive to deep scaling. When the abscess exhibits a mild cellulitis of the gingiva or when enlargement is caused by an underlying proliferative granulation tissue, pocket closure is less apt to occur as a result of deep scaling alone.

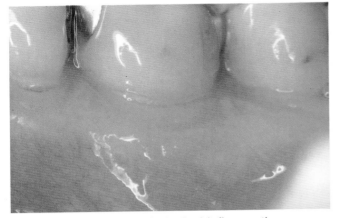

Fig. 3-10a Absence of gingival inflammation or contour changes overlying a 7-mm bifurcation involvement of the facial surface of tooth 19.

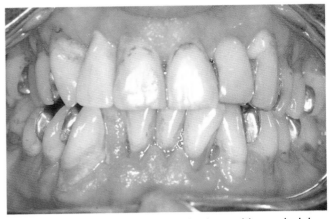

Fig. 3-10b Thick, fibrous gingiva with underlying periodontal pockets.

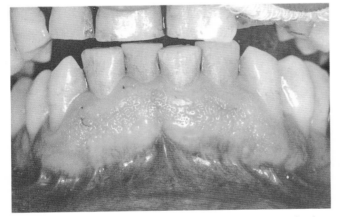

Fig. 3-10c Altered passive eruption leaves gingiva high on the crowns.

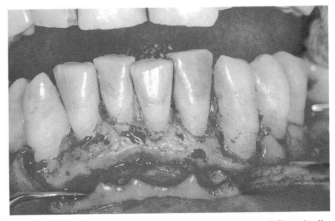

Fig. 3-10d A full-thickness mucoperiosteal flap indicates normal level of thick alveolar bone and the extent of crown coverage. Courtesy of Dr. N. Habeeb.

Areas of failure that require other therapy

Tissue characteristics: responses to irritants

Gingivitis

Gingivitis caused by systemic or noncorrectable local factors will not respond to deep scaling and root planing to an acceptable degree. Conditions such as hormonally induced desquamative gingivitis, hyperplasia due to phenytoin (Dilantin) sensitivity, gingival inflammation

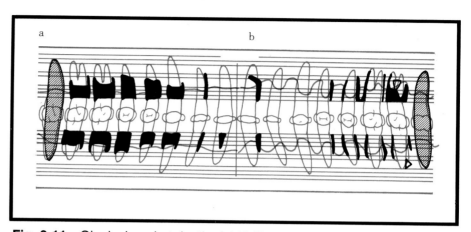

Fig. 3-11 Gingival pocket depth: *(a)* Uniform pocket depth around teeth is amenable to shrinkage if gingiva is inflamed. *(b)* Deeper proximal pockets and shallow or nonexistent facial and lingual pockets will not shrink appreciably after deep scaling. Surgical intervention should be contemplated.

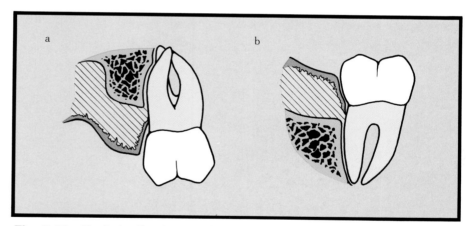

Fig. 3-12 Pockets distal to terminal molars will usually not be reduced by definitive deep scaling: *(a)* In the maxillary molars the thick fibrous tissue overlying the tuberosity will not shrink. *(b)* The mucosal tissue distal to mandibular molars is elastic and thus not subject to shrinkage. The anatomy of the area will also dictate some soft tissue regrowth even after excision.

resulting from reduced salivary flow, or the drying effects of mouth breathing are examples of tissue reactions most resistant to treatment by deep scaling along (Figs. 3-9a to d).

Periodontitis

Periodontitis that exhibits little gingival inflammation or has thick, fibrous gingiva overlying the pockets is relatively resistant to effective treatment by deep scaling and root planing. In the absence of inflammation, little pocket reduction by tissue shrinkage can occur. Reattachment of the gingival tissue is an unlikely prospect in those cases.

Predictable Results from Definitive Deep Scaling

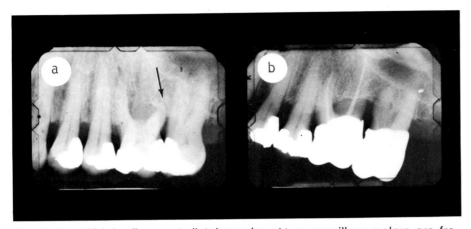

Fig. 3-13 Widely divergent distobuccal roots on maxillary molars are frequently in close proximity to the mesial roots of the adjacent tooth: *(a)* Extensive bone loss may result. *(b)* Root amputation eliminates the difficult problem.

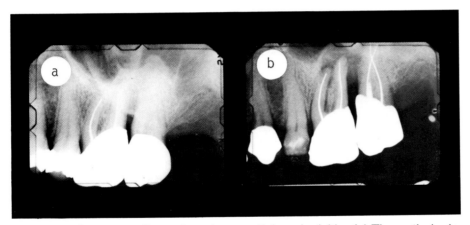

Fig. 3-14 Long-standing subacute necrotizing gingivitis: *(a)* The pathologic condition induced severe soft tissue and bony cratering in the molar areas. *(b)* Deep scaling had no affect on the pathologic condition, and even repeated surgery did not halt progress of the disease.

The uninflamed gingival tissue is frequently fibrous and thick, sometimes extending more coronally than would be expected. Some cases with thick uninflamed gingiva overlying pockets may represent a delayed passive eruption of the teeth. The gingival height will remain unchanged after scaling. Thick alveolar processes will provide tooth housings that result in infrabony defects on most root surfaces with disease. Frequently, gingiva overlying these defects show little or nor inflammation and undergo no reduction in height with deep scaling. Even in cases of thick gingiva where considerable gingival inflammation is found adjacent to the tooth, little pocket reduction will

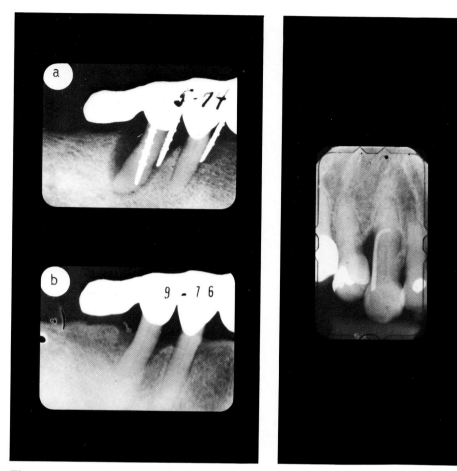

Fig. 3-15 Rapid bone destruction: *(a)* associated acute granulation-type lesions similar to Figs. 1-27a to c, *(b)* regrowth of bone after surgical excision. Courtesy of Dr. L. Hirschfeld.

Fig. 3-16 Circuitous pocket demonstrated by gutta percha point extending from distal to mesial side at base of a pocket that had a narrow entry. A mucoperiosteal flap procedure would be required to eliminate deposits at its base.

occur because of the bulk of fibrous uninflamed gingiva. In all such instances, it is well to consider surgical pocket reduction as the primary therapy (Figs. 3-10a to d).

Failure based on pocket location and configuration

1. Pockets that extend into the bifurcation or trifurcation area of molars or premolars, especially of grades II and III, will not respond to deep scaling by shrinkage or reattachment.

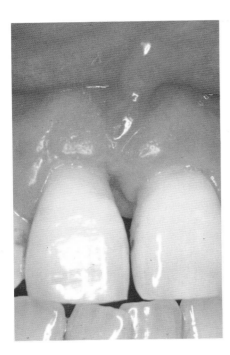

Fig. 3-17 Postsurgical recession in the anterior segment of a young woman aged 26 years. The recession was esthetically unacceptable.

2. Deep proximal pockets associated with shallow or nonexistent facial or lingual pockets on premolars and molars will respond poorly (Fig. 3-11).
3. The retromolar areas in the mandible and the thick gingiva of the tuberosity of the maxilla will undergo little shrinkage because of the nature of the adjacent anatomic structures (Fig. 3-12).
4. Deep, interdental bony craters associated with closely approximating roots in periodontitis cases have poor prospects. The most frequent area of the dentition that exhibits this change is the space between the distobuccal root of the maxillary first molar and the mesiobuccal root of the second molar. Though only the interdental soft tissue is present, the tissues are supported by the adjacent normal attachment levels on the buccal and lingual surfaces and will undergo only slight tissue shrinkage. Deep scaling usually causes only slight tissue reduction with no reattachment (Fig. 3-13).
5. In cases of long-standing subacute necrotizing gingivitis, deep and wide gingival and bony craters develop in the molar areas. These craters do not readily exhibit soft tissue regeneration as occurs elsewhere in the dentition. Surgical intervention is required to eliminate the defect (Fig. 3-14).
6. Rapidly formed pockets with attendant extensive bone loss caused by root fractures and granulation tissue enlargements are best treated by extraction and surgical excision, respectively. The rapid granulation lesion is best enucleated down to the alveolar bone using a flap procedure to provide access (Fig. 3-15).

7. Deep pockets of more than 7 mm on any tooth surface as well as those difficult to completely scale because of their anatomy will persist. These latter pockets are frequently circuitous or considerably wider at their base than at the gingival margin. Open scaling of the root surfaces is the preferred treatment (Fig. 3-16).

Deep scaling as sole therapeutic modality

In addition to those areas amenable to treatment with deep scaling because of excellence of results, a number of situations make it mandatory to use deep scaling as the sole therapeutic modality. In many of these cases, surgical intervention would be the preferred therapy, but definitive deep scaling may be the only logical or acceptable therapy. Such circumstances include:

1. Very aged individuals
2. Medically compromised patients who cannot sustain the trauma of surgery
3. Psychologically unprepared patients who cannot accept the psychic implications inherent in surgical techniques that are essentially excisional
4. Esthetic considerations where severe recession in anterior segments would be unacceptable (Fig. 3-17)
5. Extremely advanced cases wherein pocket eradication by surgery would be impossible and where extractions of many teeth and restorations are unacceptable to the patient

When such compromise therapy is completed, maintenance of the case with residual pocket depth requires very frequent recall scalings and careful supervision.

Summary

It is apparent that the effectiveness of root scaling and planing in treatment of periodontitis will vary according to tissue reactivity, pocket location, depth, and distribution, as well as a multitude of additional factors. The decision to use definitive deep scaling in some areas of an affected dentition and presurgical scaling elsewhere can usually be made at the diagnosis and treatment planning session. Goals for each form of therapy can thus be established in a planned, efficient manner.

It is rare that even a moderately advanced periodontitis can be totally treated by definitive deep scaling and root planing. Some surgical pocket elimination or compromise acceptance of pocket depths which may be difficult to stabilize is usual. It is equally rare that all areas of the dentition in such cases will require surgical pocket elimination.

References

Baderstein, A., et al. Effect of non-surgical periodontal therapy. VI. Localization of sites with probing attachment loss. J. Clin. Periodontol. 12:351, 1985.

Hakkarainen, K., et al. Influence of overhanging posterior tooth restorations on alveolar bone height in adults. J. Clin. Periodontol. 7:114, 1980.

Hughes, T.P., et al. Gingival changes following scaling, root planing and oral hygiene. J. Periodontol. 49:245, 1978.

Lovdal, A., et al. Combined effect of subgingival scaling and controlled oral hygiene on the incidence of gingivitis. Acta Odontol. Scand. 19:537, 1960.

Maury, F. Treatise on Dental Art. Philadelphia: Lea and Blanchard, 1843.

Slots, J., et al. Periodontal therapy in humans. I. Microbiological and clinical effects of a single course of periodontal scaling and root planing and of adjunctive tetracycline therapy. J. Periodontol. 50:495, 1979.

Tagge, D.L., et al. The clinical and histological response of periodontal pockets to root planing and oral hygiene. J. Periodontol. 46:527, 1975.

Torfason, T., et al. Clinical improvement of gingival conditions following ultrasonic versus hand instrumentation of periodontal pockets. J. Clin. Periodontol. 6:165, 1979.

Chapter 4

Instruments for Scaling and Planing

Since ancient times when dental therapists recognized the importance of removal of calculus and materia alba (dental plaque) as a treatment for gum disease, instruments were specifically designed to affect the procedure. Tooth scalers and "scalper medicinalis" were used by the Romans since the time of Celsus, who suggested that stains on teeth be scraped away. An elaborate set of 14 double-ended instruments was used by Albucasis (936–1013 A.D.), a Moorish physician. These instruments were primarily hooks or straight and slightly curved gravers (chisel-like scrapers). As with all instruments, they had three distinct sections: handle, shank, and sharpened blade (Fig. 4-1).

The advancing abilities of instrument makers, coupled with the ingenuity of dental practitioners, have provided the present practitioner with a multitude of instrument designs capable of reaching nearly every portion of the dentition. In the past, complete sets of instruments frequently included so many variations of angulation and were so numerous as to preclude their general use. However, some of the more efficient instruments from these sets have withstood the test of long-term use and now appear and reappear in newly created instrument sets. Though specific instruments are described in the text, similar ones that satisfy the same requirements may be readily available and may thus be substituted.

The purpose of scaling and root planing is to eliminate both supra-gingival and subgingival calculus from tooth surfaces and to create a smooth, nonirritating and chemically compatible tooth surface to interface with the gingival tissues. Since gross deposits can accumulate on the coronal surfaces and immediately below the gingival margin, heavy instruments of special designs are used for calculus removal in these areas.

Below the gingival margin, calculus, though usually less heavily deposited, may be very tenacious since it is retained by its close adaptation and even penetration into irregularities in the root surface. Access limitations within the periodontal pocket require smaller sturdy instruments, which in use have chipping, scraping, and crushing actions. The size and design of the instruments will dictate their areas of use and effectiveness.

Coronal and immediate subgingival scalers include pick scalers, prophylaxis chisels, hoes, and heavy curettes.

Subgingival scaling is best accomplished by hoes, files, and delicately proportioned curettes.

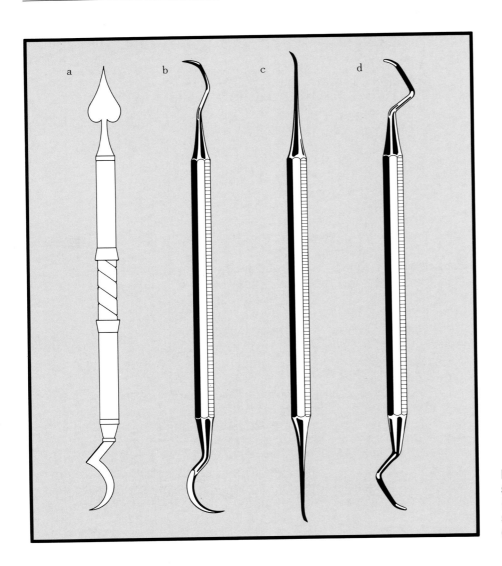

Fig. 4-1 Ancient and modern scaling instruments: *(a)* graver (Albucasis), *(b)* Jacquette pick scaler, *(c)* Zerfing prophylaxis chisel, *(d)* curette.

Pick scalers

Pick scalers characteristically have pointed, tipped, heavy blades with a triangular or trapezoidal cross section (Fig. 4-2). All edges of the blade are sharpened and are effective in shearing calculus.

The instrument can be used in either a pull or push stroke. The sharp point can insinuate itself below the calculus, splitting it from the teeth and being, therefore, useful in cleansing narrow embrasures adjacent to contact points. The scalers vary in shape from a simple sickle to multiangled instruments for use in the posterior segments. Examples of these are the Darby-Perry sickle and the McCall scalers 11 and 12, respectively.

The sides of the blades of pick scalers are either straight or convex when they are viewed from above the flat of the blade. The lateral flat or convex cutting edges reduce the area of effective contact with convex or concave proximal root surfaces (Fig. 4-3).

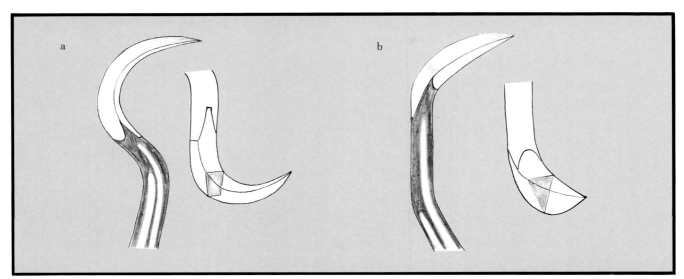

Fig. 4-2 Pick scaler: *(a)* Darby-Perry scaler with trapezoid blade, *(b)* Jacquette-type scaler with triangular blade.

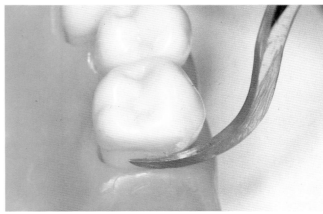

Fig. 4-3 The straight sides of pick scaler blades making limited contact on convex surfaces of a root.

Prophylaxis chisels

These end-cutting instruments are similar to their counterparts used in operative dentistry. They have straight or gently curved shanks, which end in a broader, thin, end-sharpened blade (Fig. 4-4). The design limits the chisel to use on proximal surfaces in the anterior and premolar segments. By leading the sharp edge along the crown or root surface in a carefully controlled push stroke from the facial to lingual surface, heavy supragingival deposit is readily sheared off the tooth (Fig. 4-5). Facioproximal line angles can be negotiated on anterior teeth, but special attention must be paid to avoid tissue laceration. Root concavities and sharply angled cementoenamel junctions require special care to avoid gouging the root surfaces.

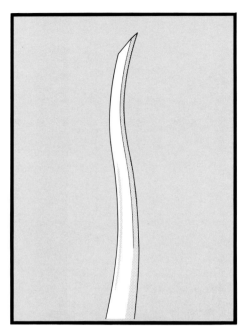

Fig. 4-4 Zerfing prophylaxis chisel.

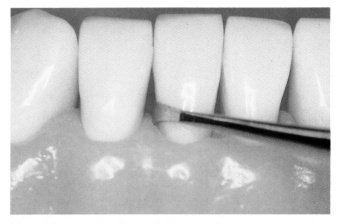

Fig. 4-5 Application of the Zerfing chisel on the proximal surface of an anterior tooth.

Hoe scalers

Periodontal hoes have broad use and, depending on the size, can negotiate the full depth of periodontal pockets. The instrument is shaped much like a garden hoe with a double-angled shank. The lip of the hoe that carries the blade is set at somewhat more than a 90-degree angle to the shank. The hoe blade is end sharpened at a 45-degree angle to the inner side of the lip (Fig. 4-6). Many hoes include a slight convex curve on the blade side of the lower shank. This curve provides a second guiding contact with the tooth crown during subgingival scaling. The length of the lip of the hoe will determine the apical extent of delivery of the instrument subgingivally. Heavy hoes are very effective in removing the thick ridge of subgingival calculus that frequently occurs just below the gingival margin. The hoe and its companion instrument the file are designed with blades set at intervals of either 90 or 45 degrees in relation to the handle. Thus, a set of eight hoes or files will reach all the proximal and faciolingual surfaces as well as all line angles of a tooth. A set of four hoes or files will reach all axial surfaces. Note that because of the proximal contact, proximal surfaces are scaled at an angle to the long axis of the tooth (Fig. 4-7).

The instrument tends to bridge radicular surface grooves and should be followed by curettes to smooth the surfaces and to scale concave areas of the root as well as the deepest portion of the pocket. Working strokes with both hoes and files should be in over-

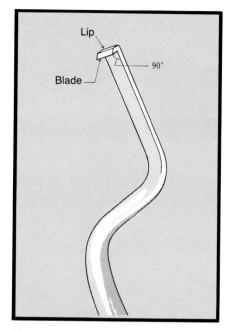

Fig. 4-6 Hoe scaler indicating lip and blade. The angle between the lip and shank is somewhat more than 90 degrees.

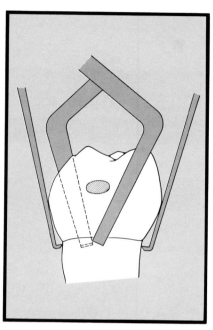

Fig. 4-7 Hoe scalers positioned around the full circumference of a tooth. Note the angled position for proximal surface placement necessitated by the contact area.

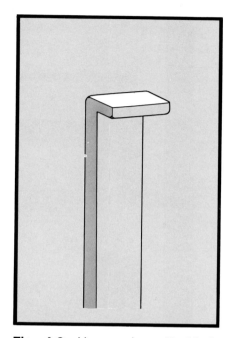

Fig. 4-8 Hoe scaler with blade edge rounded to reduce root gouging.

lapped steps so that no area is left unscaled. The sharp outer edges of the hoe should be rounded to reduce scarring of the root surface (Fig. 4-8).

Files

Periodontal files are essentially a series of very narrow hoes. They are significantly thinner than other periodontal instruments and are essentially subgingival scalers and planers. The lead edge is tapered and permits easy penetration of tightly adapted or narrow pockets (Fig. 4-9).

The file must be used carefully with strokes only in the direction of the long axis of the shank to avoid sidewise skating of the instrument blade and consequent scarring of the roots. Since the shank is thin and round, the instrument is somewhat more maneuverable than hoes. The file is less popular now, mainly because the simple technique for maintaining sharpness is not well known. However, it is an invaluable instrument in the treatment of narrow pockets, pockets on narrow-rooted teeth, deep distal pockets on molars, and pockets extending over the line angles of root surface. In addition to scaling of deposits, the file can be used to crush thin, adherent calculus for subsequent easy removal. Overlapped strokes produce smooth root surfaces.

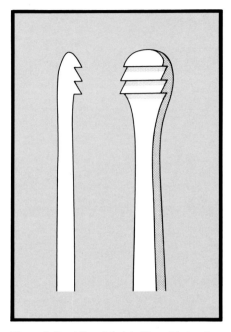

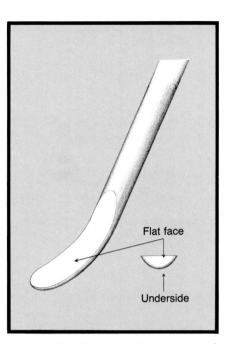

Fig. 4-9 Hirschfeld file. Note tapered lead edge and delicate proportions.

Fig. 4-10 Curette. Note curved blade sharpened all around the tip. The cross section is characteristically semilunar.

Curettes

Periodontal curettes are by far the most useful instruments for deep scaling and have no peer for root planing. Large-sized curettes are excellent for removal of heavy deposits close to the gingival margin. The smaller-sized curettes are available in a wide variety of angulations, which makes nearly all root surfaces accessible.

Curettes have curved blades that are semilunar in cross section. The flattened upper surface of the blade face has cutting edges that extend along the sides and around the rounded tip. The face of the blade makes approximately a 70-degree angle with the tangent to the rounded underside of the blade (Fig. 4-10). It is essential that this angle be maintained when the instrument is sharpened.

When most curettes are viewed from the tip of the instrument, the face of the blade is usually cut at approximately a 90-degree angle to the shank. For scaling and planing, both sides of the curette are individually usable in a pull stroke. These curettes are therefore deemed extended utility instruments that can be used on a number of surfaces of a given tooth. An exception to this design are the Gracey curettes, originally designed to be used with a push stroke. The Gracey instruments have recently been modified for use with the pull stroke. Their blades are cut at a 45-degree angle to the shank (Fig. 4-11). Only the edge farthest from the shank is generally used. They are therefore specific utility instruments, which for some instruments may limit use to a single-tooth surface.

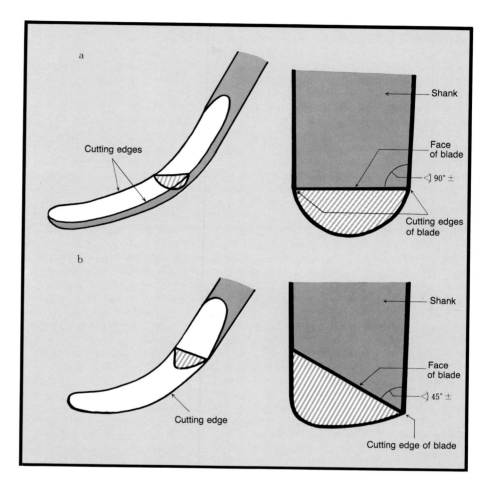

Fig. 4-11 Extended utility curettes compared with limited utility curettes (Gracey): *(a)* Extended utility curette blades have their face at a 90-degree angle to the shank and have two cutting edges. *(b)* Gracey curette blades are at a 45-degree angle to the shank. Only one cutting edge is used.

When viewed from above, the face of the blade of extended utility curettes is straight. The Gracey curettes curve away from the cutting edge in the terminal third of the blade near the tip (Fig. 4-12).

When a pull stroke is used, the face of the curette blade should make an angle of 50 to 85 degrees with the root surface. For the push stroke, the angulation must be below 45 degrees for most effective calculus removal (Fig 4-13).

When Gracey specific utility instruments are used for both posterior proximal surfaces, aligning the terminal shank with the long axis of the tooth will angle the blade correctly against the root (Fig. 4-14). Mesial and distal surfaces require different instruments. For extended utility instruments, mesial surfaces are approached similarly to the Gracey instrument, with the shank parallel to the long axis of the tooth. However, when a distal surface of the same tooth is scaled, the terminal shank-to-tooth angle changes position by 16 to 20 degrees (Figs. 4-15a and b).

The portion of the curette blade that makes contact with the tooth

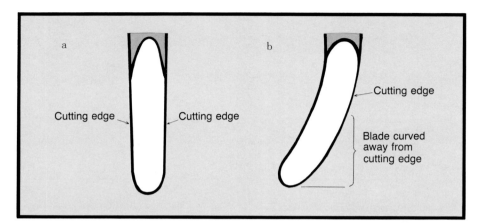

Fig. 4-12 Extended utility curettes: *(a)* and Gracey curettes, *(b)* viewed from above the face. The extended utility curette blade is straight, whereas the blade of the Gracey instrument has a curve away from the cutting edge near the tip.

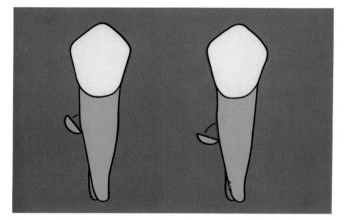

Fig. 4-13 Angulation of the face of the blade in push and pull strokes. Push *(left)* 25 to 45 degrees; pull *(right)* 60 to 85 degrees.

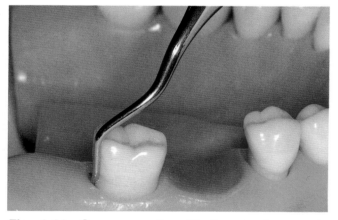

Fig. 4-14 Gracey curette with the shank properly aligned for scaling. The shank is parallel to the long axis of the tooth.

surface varies according to the root surface contours. It is rare that the curette will conform to a large area of root surface. However, closing the angle between the face of the blade and the root surface will sometimes increase the area of instrument contact (Figs. 4-16a and b). Usually only 1 or 2 mm of the blade adjacent to the tip is used. In root grooves and concavities, only the rounded tip may be effective.

When one considers the depth of subgingival penetration of the blade tip in relation to pocket width, the length and angulation of the curette blade become critically important. The longer the blade and the more closely the terminal shank angle approaches 90 degrees, the longer the horizontal profile of the instrument blade as it enters

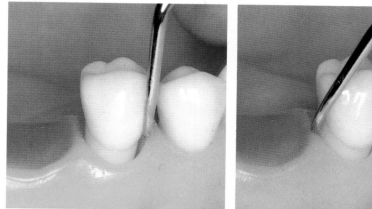

Fig. 4-15a McCall curette (extended utility) with the shank parallel to the long axis of the tooth for scaling mesial surfaces of posterior teeth.

Fig. 4-15b Angulation of McCall curette for scaling distal surfaces. The shank is 20 degrees off the long axis to produce the proper blade angle.

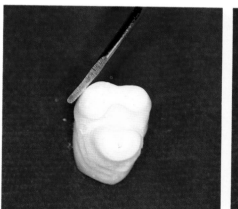

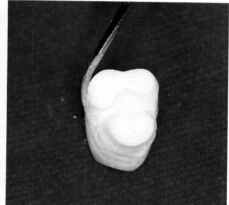

Fig. 4-16a Blade in contact with a convex root is limited when the face of the blade is open (angle of root to blade is close to 85 degrees).

Fig. 4-16b Face of blade is closed (angle of root to blade is close to 60 degrees), making possible more contact of the blade with the convex root.

the pocket. Comparison of the length and blade to shank angle of McCall 4R to that of Gracey 13 shows that the profile of the latter is obviously greater (Fig. 4-17). In addition, as is usually the case, the width of molar crowns and proximal contact areas prevents parallel placement of the instrument shank. The shank is usually angled away from the long axis of the tooth. The tip of the blade instrument is thus tilted coronally (Figs. 4-18a and b). The instrument with the terminal shank angle at or near 90 degrees will then have greater difficulty entering and negotiating the full depth of a proximal pocket. In deep proximal pockets as well as shallower but narrow-mouthed pockets on proximal surfaces, the lesser-angled instrument is preferable.

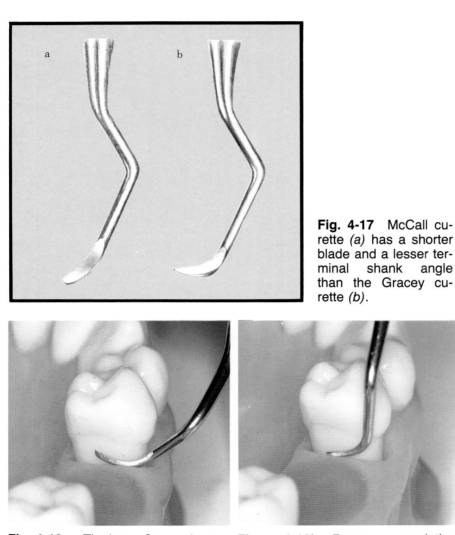

Fig. 4-17 McCall curette *(a)* has a shorter blade and a lesser terminal shank angle than the Gracey curette *(b)*.

Fig. 4-18a Tipping a Gracey instrument away from the long axis of the tooth causes the instrument tip to tilt coronally, making penetration of the pocket difficult.

Fig. 4-18b Proper angulation where possible alleviates this difficulty, though the blade length may be a deterrant to complete penetration of a narrow pocket.

Penetration of the blade tip to the base of labial and lingual pockets may be difficult using extended utility curettes in a conventional approach. In many instances, the full pocket depth can be negotiated by placing the blade at or near the long axis of the tooth. For this purpose, the longer and more acutely angled blade is preferable. An advantage in treating facial or lingual pockets on flared roots results from the curve of the Gracey curette blade in its final third. When the toe of the curved blade is in contact with the root, the shank of the instrument is tilted away from the tooth, avoiding interference by the crown (Fig. 4-19).

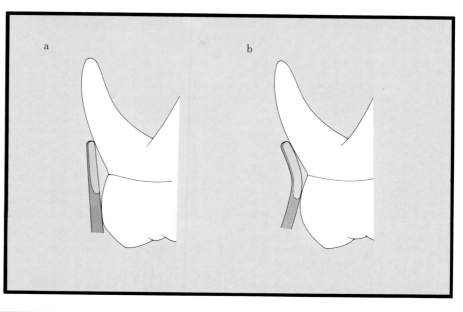

Fig. 4-19 Instrument root contact: *(a)* McCall instrument making poor root contact on a flared root when used in a horizontal stroke. *(b)* Gracey instrument makes good root contact and clears the crown in a similar stroke.

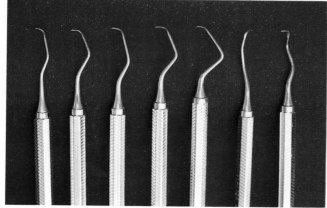

Fig. 4-20 Gracey instrument set 1 to 14.

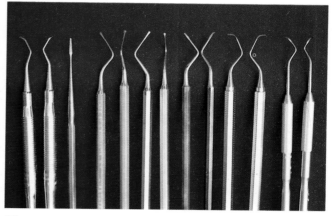

Fig. 4-21 Instrument set I use: McCall 11 and 12 pick scalers; Zerfing chisel; Hirschfeld files 3, 11, 7, and 5; McCall 4R and 4L; Gracey 7 and 8; and Goldman-Fox 3.

Though most subgingival calculus can be readily removed with fine curettes, heavy and tenacious calculus is difficult to remove because of the resilience of these fine instruments. For just such circumstances, heavy curettes are incorporated into most sets. Use of files or hoes, followed by curettes, will frequently effect removal of tenacious deposits.

Each instrument set has prescribed instruments for efficient use in different areas of the dentition. Some examples are Gracey 1 to 6 for anterior teeth and premolars, 7 and 8 for the facial and lingual surfaces of posterior teeth, 11 and 12 for the mesial surface of mo-

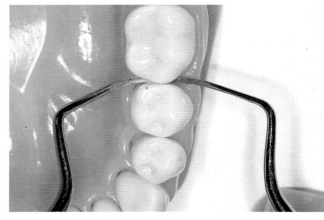

Fig. 4-22 Paired curettes for use on a proximal surface. One is used in the facial approach; the other is used in the lingual approach.

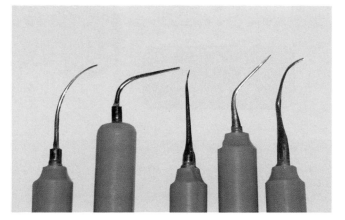

Fig. 4-23 Ultrasonic tips of different shapes are useful to accommodate various tooth surfaces.

lars, and 13 and 14 for the distal surface of posterior teeth (Fig. 4-20) and McCall 2R and 2L for anterior teeth and distal surfaces of molars, 4R and 4L for posterior teeth, and 13 and 14 for the facial, lingual, and mesial surfaces of posterior teeth. The instruments I use are the McCall 11 and 12 scalers and 4R and 4L curettes; Hirschfeld 1, 3, 5, 7, and 11 files; Gracey 7 and 8 curettes; and Goldman-Fox 3 curettes (Fig. 4-21).

Each instrument pair is intended for use on the same tooth surface, one from the facial approach and the other from the lingual approach (Fig. 4-22).

It should be noted that Gracey curettes 1 to 10 have their blades set in line with the shank and at approximately 90 degrees to the handle. Thus, the most effective strokes made with these instruments are limited to a direction closely parallel to the long axis of the handle. For the multibend Gracey 11 and 12 and 13 and 14, the direction of stroke must be made parallel to the terminal shank adjacent to the blade. Though this limitation of stroke reduces the versatility of these instruments, it simplifies instruction in their use.

The extended utility instruments, such as the McCall 4R and 4L and the 2R and 2L, have their blades set at a 100- to 110-degree angle to the line of the shank and have different angulations in relation to the handle. The stroke direction in relation to the tooth varies with placement. However, in all circumstances, the stroke direction should be as near to right angles to the face of the blade as possible.

Ultrasonic scalers

The discovery that high-frequency oscillation of an object in a fine abrasive slurry could be used to cut intricate concavities in hard objects led to the development of the dental Cavitron* machine. An unexpected offshoot of that unsuccessful device was the ultrasonic scaler, which is now an important addition to the dental armamentarium. The ultrasonic instruments vary from one brand to another, but they all consist of a high-frequency generating unit, water supply, magnetostrictor, and probelike or curette-shaped tips. The high-frequency current (26 Hz) induces mechanical shortening and lengthening of the magnetostrictor, which is connected to the water-cooled tip. A number of ingenious internal and external water flow tips have been designed (Fig. 4-23).

When used, the oscillating tip is passed over the tooth surface approximately six times in each location, overlapping and crosshatching the movements. Contact with calculus induces a vibration in the calculus that differs from that of the tooth and results in fracture of the bond holding the calculus. A scraping action on stain is also effective in stain removal.

The major disadvantage to the ultrasonic scaler is the thickness of the tips and the lack of balance and weight of the handpiece. The scaler must be stopped to determine the presence of remaining accretions. Therefore, after ultrasonic scaling, the surfaces should be checked with a sharp curette. Soft tissue debridement using sharper curette-like inserts is also possible.

References

Baderstein, A., et al. Effect of non-surgical periodontal therapy in moderately advanced periodontitis. J. Clin. Periodontol. 8:57, 1981.

D'Silva, I.V., et al. An evaluation of root topography following periodontal instrumentation—a scanning electron microscopic study. J. Periodontol. 50:283, 1979.

Ewen, S.J., et al. A scanning electron microscopic study of teeth following periodontal instrumentation. J. Periodontol. 48:92, 1977.

Hirschfeld, I. The "Presurgical Era" in Periodontal Therapy. Lecture. Massachusetts State Dental Soc. 1964.

Nishime, D., et al. Hand instrumentation versus ultrasonics in the removal of endotoxin from root surfaces. J. Periodontol. 50:345, 1979.

Orban B., et al. A macroscopic and microscopic study of instruments designed for root planing. J. Periodontol. 27:120, 1956.

Pattison, G.L., et al. Periodontal Instrumentation: A Clinical Manual. Reston, Va.: Reston Publ. Co., Inc., 1979.

Weinberger, B.W. An Introduction to the History of Dentistry. St. Louis: The C.V. Mosby Co., 1948.

Wilkinson, R.F., et al. Scanning electron microscope of the root surface following instrumentation. J. Periodontol. 44:559, 1973.

*Dentsply International, York, Pa.

Chapter 5

Instrument Maintenance

The sense of root roughness, so important to detection of subgingival calculus, is most efficiently transmitted by the passage of a sharp edge or point across the root surface. As an instrument blade becomes dull and rounded, the detecting edge no longer defines root surface characteristics. Rather, only contour changes, diagnostic for calculus but inadequate for root surface roughness, are indicated. For this reason, and also because sharp-edged instruments are mandatory for efficient calculus removal, constant attention must be paid to the condition of the cutting edges of the instrument in hand.

Instrument sharpening

It is not unusual to find that instrument sharpening may be required during a single session of deep scaling. The operator will first notice a loss of bite of the instrument on the root surface; then detection of root roughness will become more difficult. At such times the instrument should be tested for sharpness by applying the blade at a working angle to a smooth-surfaced plastic rod (Figs. 5-1a to c). The blade should engage and nick the surface of the root with minimal pressure. If the blade slips along the plastic surface, the edge requires sharpening. Alternatively, the edge of the blade should be viewed by reflecting light. If a reflective edge is seen, the instrument is dull.

   The objective of sharpening an instrument is to reestablish a cutting edge with the original angles and contours of the blade. The tools used for sharpening are:

1. Flat hand-held hones of various grits (e.g., the medium India, fine Arkansas, or fine ceramic)
2. Rounded, edged, hand-held hones of similar grits
3. Mounted cylindrical ruby stones
4. The Neivert whittler,* which is a mounted tungsten carbide blade with one square and one rounded edge
5. A modified jeweler's slitting file in which the original diamond-shaped cross section is altered by thinning (Figs. 5-2a to c)

*Temrex, Div. Interstate Dental Co., Inc., Freeport, N.Y.

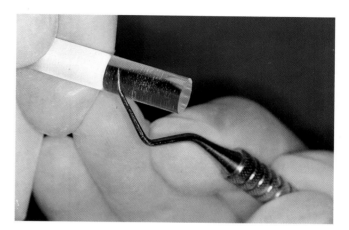

Fig. 5-1a Testing the cutting edge on an acrylic rod.

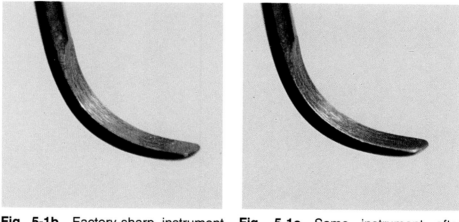

Fig. 5-1b Factory-sharp instrument cutting edge shows no reflection at instrument blade cutting edge.

Fig. 5-1c Same instrument after 125 strokes on root surface exhibits reflected light at now dulled cutting edge.

Serum hepatitis

A word of caution must be introduced at this point concerning the possible innoculation of serum hepatitis virus directly by infected instruments and indirectly by infected sharpening tools. The disease is now so widespread that the precaution of autoclaving all instruments and tools is mandatory. Abrasive hones, which require an oiled surface, cannot be autoclaved with such coatings and should be moistened with water or used dry. Without oil, stones will become clogged after a period of use. When this occurs, immersion of the stone in an ultrasonic cleaning bath of a dilute calculus remover solution will rapidly restore the abrasive surface to the hones.

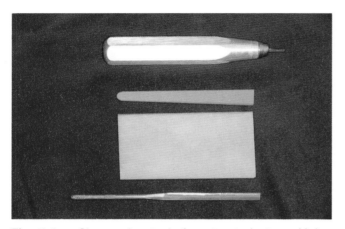

Fig. 5-2a Sharpening tools from top to bottom: Neivert whittler blade, fine India stone, Arkansas hand hone, and modified jeweler's slitting file.

Fig. 5-2b Neivert whittler blade *(left)* has sharpened cutting edges and *(right)* rounded back for burnishing.

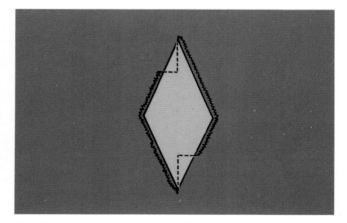

Fig. 5-2c Jeweler's slitting file in cross section: Dotted lines show areas to be ground away to make file edge thinner.

Flat-edged instruments

As a general rule, all blades are sharpened by passing abrasives toward the cutting edge, thus avoiding a burred wire edge. For all flat-edged instruments, such as hoes and chisels, the blade is set on a firmly supported stone at exactly the angle of the original cut. The instrument is drawn or pushed toward its cutting edge with the instrument braced by fingers in contact with the stone. The movement is kept short, in the range of 1 to 2 cm, since it is difficult to maintain proper instrument angulation over longer distances (Fig. 5-3).

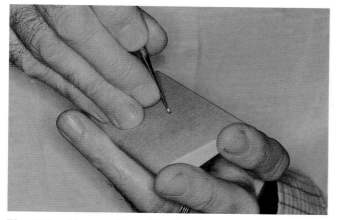

Fig. 5-3 Sharpening a Zerfing file by pushing the instrument away from the operator.

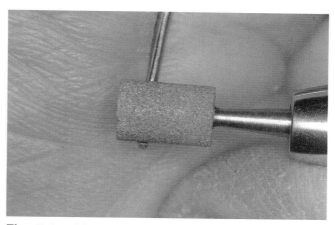

Fig. 5-4a Mounted ruby stone held flat across the face of a curette blade. Sharpening starts on the blade short of the terminal shank angle.

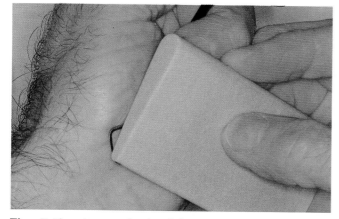

Fig. 5-4b A round-edged hand hone used across the face of a curette in very short, controlled movements.

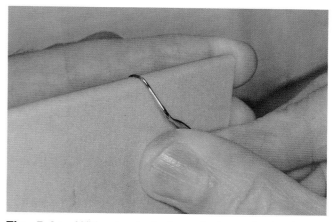

Fig. 5-4c With short strokes, the curette is drawn across a carefully braced, rounded, edged, hand hone.

Curettes and curved scalers

Curettes and curved scalers may be sharpened on either the face of the blade, sides of the blade, or both. When an instrument is wide and heavy, honing the sides of the blade will in time produce a narrower more useful instrument. However, if a curette is delicate and thin in all proportions, it is best to alternate honing of the face and sides of the blade during successive sharpenings. Since only the last few millimeters of a blade are used during deep scaling, most sharpening will be required in the tip half. It is imperative that the blade not be weakened by excessive honing of the face at the blade-to-shank junction.

Face of curette blade

The face of a curette blade is sharpened by bracing the instrument on a fixed surface or in the hand with the face horizontal and up. The tip faces toward the operator. The flat is then honed using either a slowly rotating moistened mounted stone or the curved side of a hand-held abrasive hone. Care is taken to place the stones in full contact with the horizontal surface of the blade. The fingers holding the handpiece or abrasive are braced against the hand holding the instrument. The moistened mounted stone is passed from a point short of the terminal shank angle toward the tip. The hand hone is placed with its curved edge in contact with as much of the end of the blade as possible, avoiding the final curve. A few short side to side movements are then made. The curette may also be sharpened by passing the blade along the curved side of a hand hone. The instrument must be firmly gripped and carefully placed on the curved surface of the hone, with only the terminal two thirds of the blade in contact. The thumb of the hand grasping the instrument is used as a guide as the instrument is moved approximately 5 mm in each direction. It is nearly impossible to recreate the original flat of the blade when it is sharpened by hand. A slightly two-planed "flat of the blade" is acceptable (Figs. 5-4a to c).

The Neivert whittler is more likely to maintain a single-planed surface on the face of a curette blade. With the curette hand braced, the Neivert whittler blade is angled so that one of its sharpened edges makes a 45-degree angle to the face of the curette blade. Starting short of the blade-to-shank junction, the whittler is moved toward the tip using considerable pressure. A few passes are required to remove enough metal to freshen the edge. The sides of the blade are stroked with the rounded side of the whittler to remove the wire bur (Figs. 5-5a to c).

Side of curette blade

The side of the scaler and curette blades may be sharpened by using the flat of hand-held hones or the Neivert whittler. The angle between the side and flat of the curette is critical. Therefore, the angle of the hone or whittler to the blade must be constant during sharpening. The hones are held lengthwise between the thumb and fingers. The curette is braced with the face up as the hone is passed downward past the edge in a single or series of strokes, which follow the outer curve of the blade. The vertical strokes follow around the curve of the tip of the blade, avoiding the tendency to create a pointed tip (Fig. 5-6). When the whittler is used, its blade is angled at the side to flat angle and passed along the side of the blade to the center of the tip, maintaining the original cutting angle of the curette. If the stroke of the whittler is directed downward and toward the tip, no wire bur will be produced.

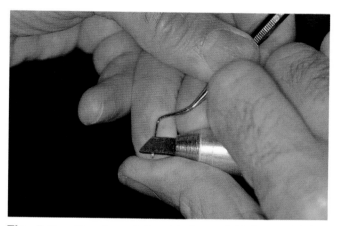

Fig. 5-5a Bracing of the blade and Neivert whittler for sharpening.

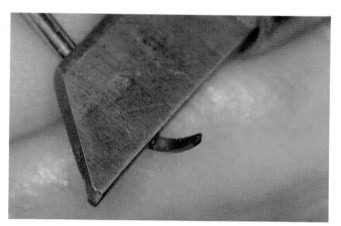

Fig. 5-5b The whittler cutting edge starts short of the terminal shank angle.

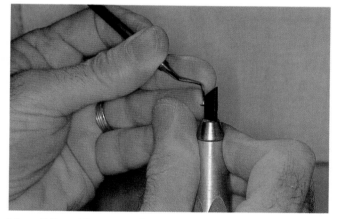

Fig. 5-5c The rounded blade of the whittler burnishes off the wire bur.

Fig. 5-6 A hand hone passing from the face to back of a curette along the side of the blade. Note that the angle of the side of the curette back must be maintained.

Files

Files are sharpened on each of the blade surfaces perpendicular to the instrument head. A modified jeweler's file is placed to the full depth of the interblade groove with its unmodified surface against the perpendicular edge. A few short, light strokes on a firmly supported instrument will be adequate to sharpen each blade (Figs. 5-7a and b).

The surfaces of various instruments that are sharpened and the direction of movement of the sharpening stones, files, and whittler are shown in Figs. 5-8a and b.

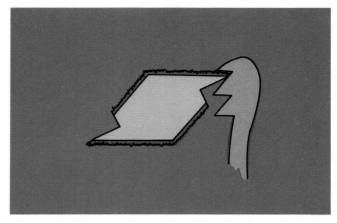

Fig. 5-7a Hirschfeld file properly braced for sharpening stroke by modified jeweler's file.

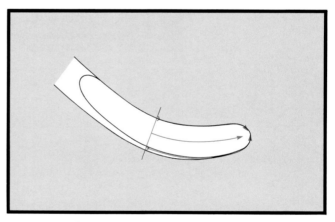

Fig. 5-7b Penetration of the thin-edged jeweler's file to the depth of the groove between the file blades.

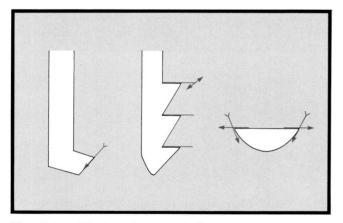

Fig. 5-8a Blade edges and direction of movement when sharpening with hones and files.

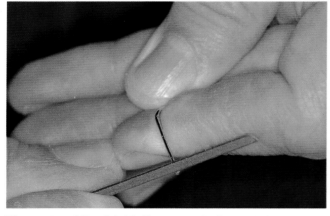

Fig. 5-8b Sharpening instrument direction when using a Neivert whittler or mounted Ruby stone.

Neivert whittler

The Neivert whittler itself has to be maintained with keen edges on its flat side. A machinist's diamond hone, grit no. 600, has a sufficiently hard and fine surface to pare down the tungsten carbide blade. The blade is held flat against a fixed hone and moved sideways over the length of the hone. The Neivert whittler blade should be tested for sharpness.

With long-term use or after poor sharpening technique, curettes may become thin, springy, or pointed. The springiness of the instrument makes calculus removal difficult since the resistance of the instrument to flexure is reduced. The pointed end will frequently pierce the soft tissue attachment, causing pain. For hoes and files, the instrument blade decreases in depth with each sharpening until the blade is too shallow to properly cut through calculus. Instruments should be replaced in anticipation of approaching ineffectiveness.

References

Antonini, C.J., et al. Scanning electron microscope study of scalers. J. Periodontol. 48:45, 1977.

DeNucci, D.J., et al. Scanning electron microscope evaluation of several resharpening techniques. J. Periodontol. 54:618, 1983.

Withers, J.A. Hepatitis—a review of the disease and its significance to dentistry. J. Periodontol. 51:162, 1980.

Chapter 6

Root Scaling and Planing Techniques

It has been established beyond any reasonable doubt that bacterial plaque and supragingival and subgingival calculus are primary etiologic agents in periodontal disease. In addition, strong evidence indicates that cementum exposed to the endotoxins of subgingival plaque is inhibitory to collagenesis and, therefore, healing of periodontal pockets. Definitive scaling and root planing procedures are designed to eliminate these etiologic and probable inhibitory agents and, consequently, to establish a local environment compatible with healing.

All deposits on root surfaces must therefore be completely removed by scaling and the root surface planed smooth in an attempt to eliminate toxic substances. What would seem to be a simple set of objectives requires one of the most difficult procedures to effectively execute as a closed procedure. Proper subgingival scaling depends on the development of a highly refined tactile sense for detection of deposits and a stabilized, forceful stroke for their removal.

Instrument grasp

While scaling, one must develop a versatility and delicacy of instrument placement and movement. Of all recommended instrument grasps, the three-finger grasp provides the widest range of movements and lightness of touch. The instrument is held in the manner of a dart, with the instrument being held between the index finger and thumb and resting alongside the ball of the third finger (Fig. 6-1).

Since the instrument is held and controlled by the three fingers, movements of the instrument can be made independently of remaining fingers. When the much used two-finger (pen) grasp is compared with the three-finger grasp, the advantages of the three-finger grasp become apparent. In the pen grasp, the instrument is firmly held by the thumb and index finger and at the first joint of the third finger. The third finger is used as the firm pivoting rest, around which all movement is made. The instrument, therefore, cannot be moved independently of the remainder of the hand, reducing its versatility of action. A thumb-index finger grasp has been recommended for re-

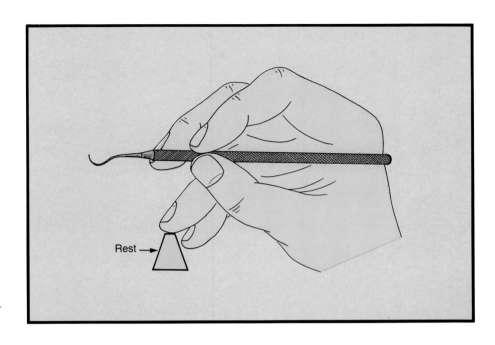

Rest →

Fig. 6-1 Three-finger instrument grasp.

moval of heavy deposit on the anterior teeth. The movements made with such an instrument grasp are limited to short, forceful working strokes. The grasp is recommended for removal of only very heavy deposit that is supragingival or immediately subgingival.

Strokes using three-finger grasp

The strokes that can be executed when using the three-finger grasp fall into four categories:

1. A linear stroke produced by flexing the grasping fingers in the direction of the long axis of the instrument (Fig. 6-2). The instrument blade will move along a relatively straight line in a highly controlled manner. Such a stroke is useful when working in narrow pockets on anterior teeth and when using files and hoes.
2. A rotating stroke produced by rolling the instrument on the third finger as the thumb and index finger turn the instrument (Fig. 6-3). The instrument blade moves along a narrow arc for a short distance. The instrument is under excellent control during a forceful stroke. The stroke is most useful on the distal surfaces of posterior teeth where instrument control is difficult.
3. A pivoting stroke using the fourth finger rest as the fulcrum for the motion. The stroke can be lateral when the forearm and hand are fixed and rotated as a unit (Fig. 6-4). The lateral stroke is used on proximal surfaces of all teeth. Also, the pivoting motion can be

Root Scaling and Planing Techniques

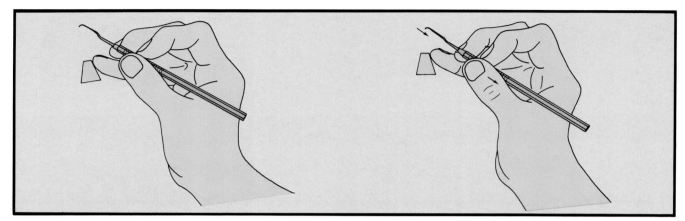

Fig. 6-2 Linear stroke: *(Left)* Start. *(Right)* All grasp fingers are flexed toward the palm.

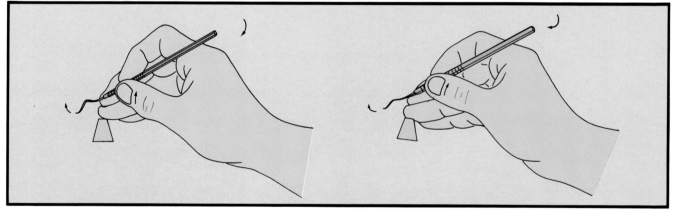

Fig. 6-3 Rotating stroke: *(Left)* Start. *(Right)* The thumb and index finger roll the instrument along the middle finger, rotating the handle and turning the blade.

Fig. 6-4 Lateral pivoting stroke: *(Left)* Start. *(Right)* Lateral rotation of hand and forearm around the fourth finger fulcrum.

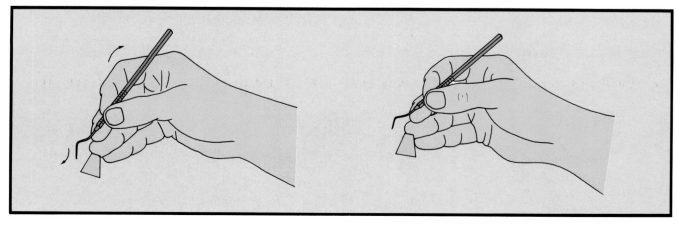

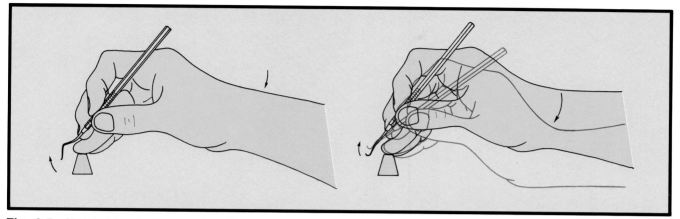

Fig. 6-5 Wrist-drip pivoting stroke: *(Left)* Start. *(Right)* Wrist drops (flexes) and hand pivots up and down on the fourth finger fulcrum.

Figs. 6a to d Stabilizing rests.

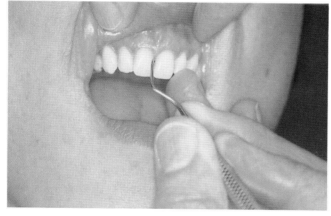

Fig. 6-6a Intraoral rest, close.

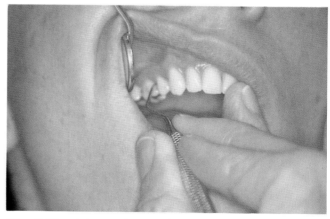

Fig. 6-6b Intra-oral rest, distant.

Fig. 6-6c Intraoral rest on finger in mucobuccal fold.

Fig. 6-6d Intraoral thumb rest.

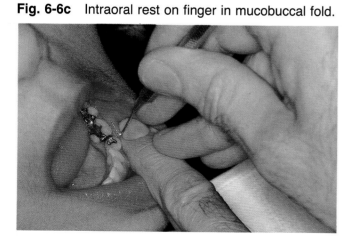

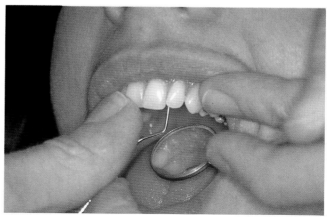

Root Scaling and Planing Techniques

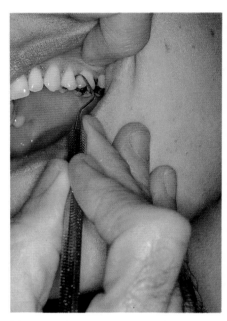

Fig. 6-7a Extraoral cheek rest.

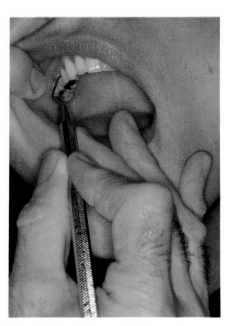

Fig. 6-7b Extraoral chin rest.

forward and backward with the hand moving up or down as the wrist is flexed (Fig. 6-5). The stroke is useful on mesial surfaces of most teeth. The arc of motion of the blade for all pivoting strokes is dependent on the distance of the instrument blade from the pivoting rest. The longer that distance, the more linear the stroke.

4. A stroke that combines in various measures components of the three other strokes. Of the four types of strokes, the combination stroke is used most frequently.

Rests

The stability of the rest and its relation to the working blade is of extreme importance. Intraoral rests are the most common. The rest fingers are stabilized on the teeth or on a finger placed in the mucobuccal fold adjacent to the lower anterior teeth (Figs. 6-6a to d). Extraoral rests are possible since the patient will brace the lower jaw when the side of the hand or fingers apply pressure to the jaw. This distancing of the rest from the working tip allows for uncramped fingers and unencumbered execution of any of the various strokes (Figs. 6-7a and b). The closer the rest to the working blade, the more apt are the strokes to be limited to the pivoting stroke. The more distant the rest from the scaling site, the more delicate the tactile stroke and the more versatile the working stroke. Control of the in-

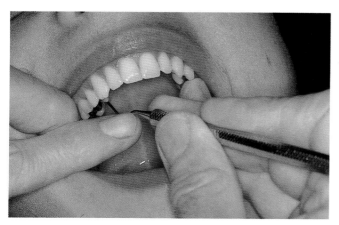

Fig. 6-8 Stabilizing instrument with index finger when rest is very distant from working site.

Figs. 6-9a and b Built-up rests desirable for use with Gracey instruments.

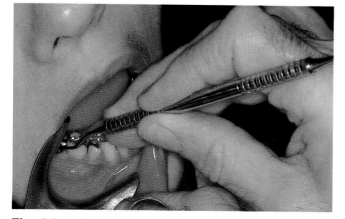

Fig. 6-9a In the lower jaw, the third finger is placed on top of fourth finger to increase handle angulation.

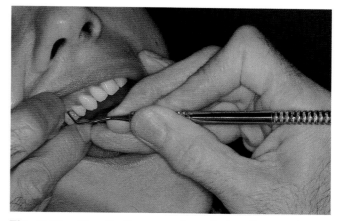

Fig. 6-9b Fourth finger rest on index finger placed on occlusal surfaces of posterior teeth to increase handle angulation.

Fig. 6-10a Planar rest.

Fig.6-10b Opposed rest.

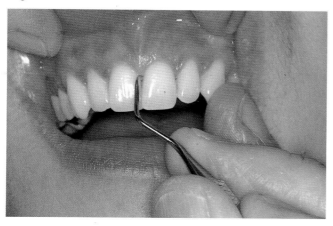

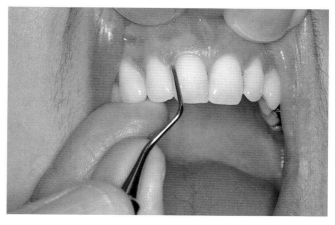

Root Scaling and Planing Techniques

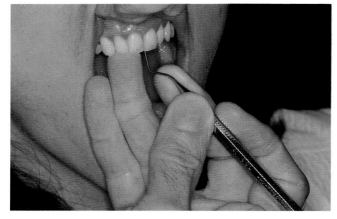

Fig. 6-11 Palm up hand placement has limiting affects on strokes.

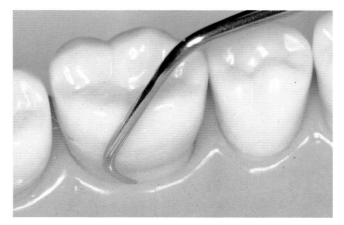

Fig. 6-12 Entry angulation of curette tip.

strument is sometimes more difficult with a distant rest, especially when the rest is across the arch. Under such circumstances, the instrument can be stabilized by either the thumb or index finger of the nonworking hand, reducing slippage (Fig. 6-8).

When Gracey instruments are used in the posterior sextants, proper access to the deepest part of the pocket requires that the instrument handle be positioned more vertically than is possible, with a rest directly on the teeth. A built-up rest is necessary and is provided for by placing the third finger on top of the fourth finger in the lower arch (Fig. 6-9a). For the upper arch, the thumb or index finger of the nonworking hand is interposed between the occlusal surface of the teeth and the usual fourth finger rest (Fig. 6-9b). The instrument movement is limited to a lateral or wrist-drop pivoting stroke.

Fatigue and tenderness of the fingers that stabilize the rest can be avoided by using a planar rather than an opposed rest relationship (Figs. 6-10a and b). In the opposed relationship, the blade is moved and controlled by movement in a direction toward the tips of the rest fingers. In a planar relationship, the rest fingers are held in a plane parallel to but not directly opposing the direction of the blade movement. Thus, the rest provides stability but allows slight movement of the fleshy parts of the rest fingers. During instrumentation, the palm of the hand usually faces down toward the patient. However, for some scaling positions, a palm-up hand position is required. The finger rest in the palm-up position is usually closer to the working site, with consequent limitation of the direction and variety of strokes (Fig. 6-11).

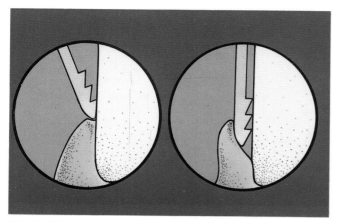

Fig. 6-13 Angulations of Hirschfeld file: *(Left)* entry, *(Right)* working.

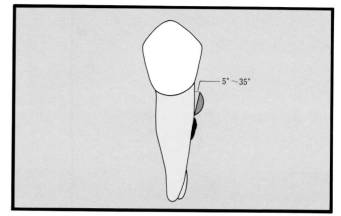

Fig. 6-14 Exploratory stroke blade angulation for greatest tactile sensation.

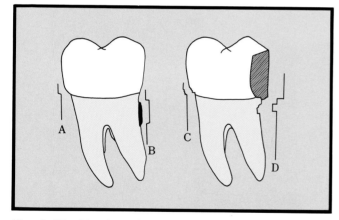

Fig. 6-15 Tooth surface characteristics as related to movement of instrument blade. (See text for identification of *A, B, C,* and *D.*)

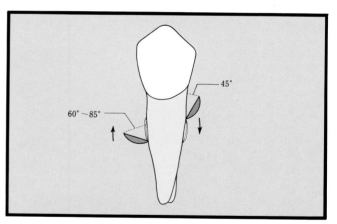

Fig. 6-16 Pull and push stroke blade angulations.

General principles in instrumentation

Having determined by observation of tissue tone and color and by periodontal probing that a pocket exists on a given tooth surface, the operator must then delineate the extent and configuration of the pocket. Should the gingival margin be tightly adapted to the tooth because of minimal inflammation, entry into the pocket may be difficult and painful. When the curette is passed subgingivally, the least distension of the margin will occur when the narrowest aspect of the side of the blade is passed between the tooth and the gingiva. This movement is accomplished by angling the curettes so that the face

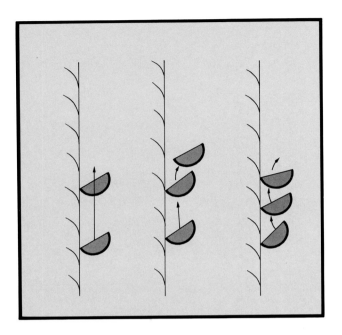

Fig. 6-17 Instrument path on root surface during working strokes: *(Left)* Linear stroke and pivoting strokes. *(Middle)* Linear strokes are best for longer planing contact. *(Right)* Rotation strokes are better for short chipping action.

of the blade is nearly parallel to the root surface and passing the lead edge of the tip subgingivally (Fig. 6-12). For the Hirschfeld files, the first angled flat of the blade is placed parallel to and in contact with the root surfaces by angling the shank away from the tooth (Fig. 6-13). Once the gingiva has become somewhat stretched by the initial entry, subsequent entries can be made easily and painlessly.

Exploratory strokes in identification of surface irregularities

During the exploratory stroke, the instrument is held very lightly so that the tactile sensitivity of the fingers is maximized. The instrument is positioned so that the flat of the blade makes a very acute angle with the root surface in the range of 5 to 35 degrees (Fig. 6-14). The lead edge of the instrument is passed along the root surface using a light contacting pressure. The presence and configuration of surface irregularities are thus readily defined. The surface of the tooth can exhibit a number of irregularities as one passes first apically and then coronally (Fig. 6-15):

1. Filling overhangs or the indentation of the cementoenamel junction, which in apically directed passage causes the instrument to move inward toward the tooth (*A*).
2. Rough excrescences of calculus, which are felt in both the apical and coronal stroke. The instrument will first move outward away from the tooth and then back (*B*).

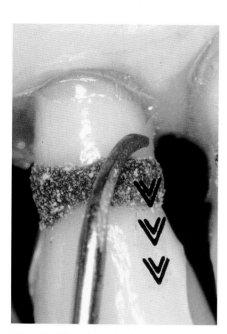

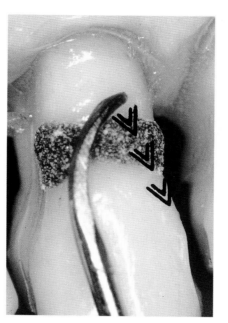

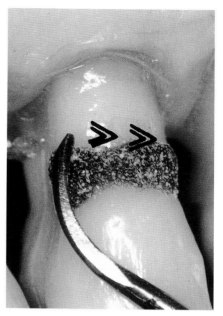

Fig. 6-18a Vertical stroke direction.

Fig. 6-18b Diagonal stroke direction.

Fig. 6-18c Horizontal stroke direction.

3. Roughness of the cervical enamel and fine slight roughness of exposed cementum *(C)*.
4. Root resorptions or cavities wherein the instrument moves inward toward the root and then outward in both stroke directions *(D)*.

The exploratory stroke is continued apicalward until the resilient soft tissue attachment is felt and its outline explored. To scale, one must change the instrument-to-tooth angle to the working angle, which is 60 to 85 degrees for a pull stroke and less than 45 degrees for a push stroke (Fig. 6-16). The instrument grasp is made firm; for pivoting strokes, the whole hand is made rigid and moves as a unit. Short chipping strokes in combination with small planing movements are made covering a small area until the calculus has been removed and the root feels smooth. The adjacent area of the root is then explored for the presence of calculus. If calculus is present, the process is repeated, making certain that the areas scaled are overlapped.

The apicalward movement of the instrument must be made after each working stroke using a gentle grasp so as not to damage the soft tissue attachment. For each pair of strokes, the instrument grasp is firmed during the working portion and eased during the apical repositioning of the instrument, preparatory to another working stroke. Exploratory strokes are then made to determine whether the calculus has been removed. To properly test for complete calculus removal, one should pass the blade over the root in a direction different from the previous strokes. Using an instrument with a different configura-

Figs. 6-19a and b Terminal shank parallel to long axis of tooth for Gracey 11 to 14.

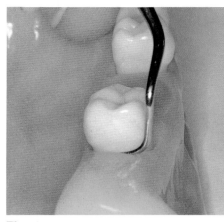

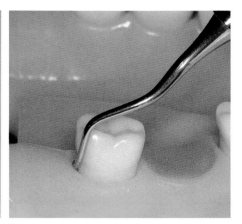

Fig. 6-19a Buccolingual view.

Fig. 6-19b Mesiodistal view.

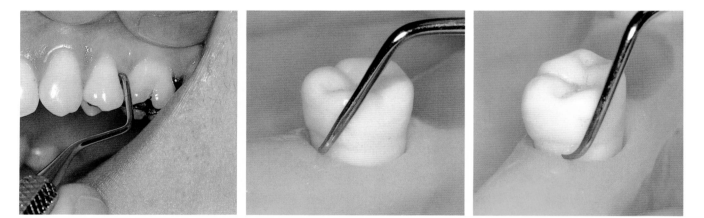

Fig. 6-20a McCall instrument shank parallel to long axis of tooth for mesial surface of posterior teeth.

Fig. 6-20b Shank angled 20 degrees toward mesial surface for distal surface scaling.

Fig. 6-20c Instrument tip rotated toward tooth to close face-to-tooth angle.

tion is helpful in locating residual calculus and root roughness. Longer planing strokes are then used to eliminate residual calculus or irregularities of the root surface.

Pull strokes may be used in the variety of strokes described. Push strokes are almost always pivotal or linear since these strokes best maintain a relatively constant blade-to-tooth angulation (Fig. 6-17). Since the blade of hoes and files is perpendicular to the long axis of the shank of the instrument, all working strokes must be in the direction of the instrument shank, no matter what the relationship to the long axis of the tooth. The pivoting and linear strokes produce the required straight-line movement of the blade. The forward and back

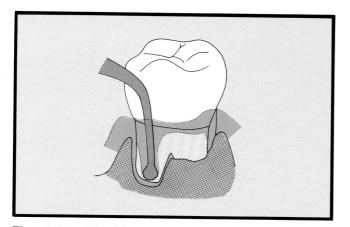

Fig. 6-21 Hirschfeld file used for scaling narrow pockets requires that the first blade be carried past the epithelial attachment.

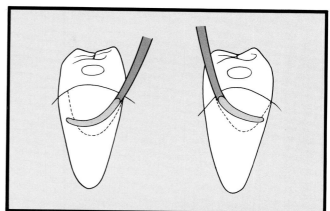

Fig. 6-22 Extension of instrument tips in a facial or lingual direction may cause laceration of the epithelial attachment.

pivoting stroke (wrist drop) produces a blade movement, which is almost straight lined when the pivoting rest is more distant from the instrument tip. Since the blade of the hoe and file is a slight distance from the instrument tip, a curette should be used to scale the most apical portion of the pocket.

The endpoint of root scaling and planing is the tactile sensation of smooth root surfaces in all directions. It is only then that one may assume that all calculus and rough-surfaced cementum have been removed.

Direction of instrument strokes

The direction of instrument strokes will vary with the instrument design, tooth anatomy, and pocket configuration. The direction of the stroke may be parallel or diagonal to the long axis of the tooth or may be circumferential to the root (Figs. 6-18a to c). For effective scaling or planing, all strokes must be perpendicular to that part of the working edge of the blade in contact with the tooth. In general, proximal surfaces are scaled using strokes approximately in the long axis of the tooth or in slight diagonals. Facial and lingual surfaces are scaled with longer-bladed instruments, such as the Gracey 7/8, using a diagonal or circumferential stroke.

Working blade to root angle. The most efficient angulation of blade-to-root surface falls within a rather wide range of 60 to 85 degrees. Unfortunately, root contours are highly varied in both an apico-occlusal and circumferential direction. The best guide for maintaining proper blade-to-root angulation is the feel of the blade engaging the root surface at the proper angle. Such a sense of feel can be developed by working on exposed root surfaces in a dentition or on an extracted tooth. Comparison of the blade angulation and the observed effectiveness of the instrument will help develop a sense for proper feel. Another guide for instrument angulation for limited utility curettes is to place the shank of such instruments as the Graceys 11/12 and 13/14 parallel to the long axis of the tooth (Figs. 6-19a and b). A similar guide for McCall 4R/4L and 2R/2L on mesial surfaces of posterior teeth is useful (Fig. 6-20a). However, if they are applied to distal surfaces, the terminal shank must be angled 20 degrees to the long axis of the tooth to provide a proper blade-to-root angulation (Fig. 6-20b). Another means of closing the blade-to-root angle of wide utility instruments is to turn the tip of the blade toward the tooth. Though the area of the blade in contact with the tooth decreases, the maneuver will produce greater penetration of the instrument into the pocket as well as better blade angulation (Fig. 6-20c).

Care must be taken to avoid laceration of the soft tissue attachment on the lateral aspect of pockets, especially when the difficult-to-control circumferential stroke is used at or near the full depth of the pocket. Since almost any circumferential movement in a narrow pocket will lacerate the soft tissues, the circumferential stroke should be reserved for wide-based pockets or for planing coronal to the full pocket depth. To reach the full depth of narrow pockets, the Hirschfeld file is most effective (Fig. 6-21). Since the first blade of the file is approximately 1 mm from the tip of the instrument, a conscious effort should be made to penetrate the epithelial attachment to scale the base of the pocket.

Similarly, when a proximal pocket is scaled, long-bladed instruments such as the Gracey 11/12 and 13/14 will engage the lingual gingiva during a buccal approach to the pocket. The buccal gingiva can be lacerated when the pocket is approached from the lingual aspect. One must be constantly vigilant and estimate the position of the instrument tip by observing the shank and its buccolingual relationship to the tooth and gingiva (Fig. 6-22).

Effects of long deep scaling sessions

During long sessions of deep scaling, the tactile sensitivity of most operators will deteriorate as the result of fatigue and pressure of the instruments on the fingers. It is best to divide scaling of a dentition into managable segments to avoid such an eventuality. Even so, it should be expected that an initial scaling of an area will be less than perfect. The scaled areas should be rechecked at subsequent visits using such indicators of incomplete scaling as residual gingival inflammation or suppuration.

Each repeated root scaling and planing probably removes a small amount of endotoxin-laden cementum. The inevitable trauma to the pocket wall during scaling, though minimized by careful instrumentation, also induces an acute inflammatory reaction in the gingiva.

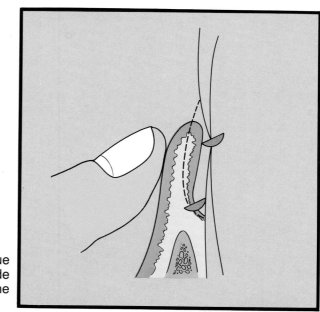

Fig. 6-23 Soft tissue curettage. Note blade is angled toward the soft tissue.

The recurrent acute inflammatory reaction and its resolution may be important factors in gingival healing and pocket closure. Portions of the sulcular and junctional epithelium are undoubtedly removed as well. The exposed underlying connective tissue in contact with endotoxin-free cementum may have the potential for reattachment to the root surface.

Ultrasonic scaling

Supragingival scaling with ultrasonic instruments of various designs is a rapid and effective means of removing heavy supragingival calculus and stain. For subgingival scaling, curette-shaped tips and straight internal flow tips are useful. A considerable number of clinical and laboratory studies indicate an equal effectiveness of ultrasonic scaling and hand instrumentation in subgingival calculus removal. Similar degrees of root damage are reported by some, whereas others find more root gouging with ultrasonic instruments. A major disadvantage to ultrasonic curettes is that the subgingival inserts are large and the handpiece itself is heavy and cumbersome, lacking any balance. Tactile sensation is impossible during use; thus, for calculus removal, a routine pattern of six to eight cross-hatched passages are made over a surface. A hand instrument should then be used to test root surfaces for completeness of calculus removal. In my experience, longitudinal calculus ridges are almost always found separated by well-scaled areas. Fortunately, the calculus is easy to detect since the ultrasonic scaler leaves the rough surface of the calculus unaltered. It has been reported that in areas of difficult instrumentation, such as molar areas, the ultrasonic scaler shows no advantage in calculus or plaque removal over hand instruments. Adequate water coolant is mandatory to avoid root damage, and the blade should be kept moving constantly and placed flat against the root surface. Though some reports indicate smooth-planed roots after ultrasonic scaling, others find it deficient for root planing. It would seem that in all instances an evaluation of surface smoothness by hand instruments would be obligatory.

Soft tissue curettage

Under those circumstances where residual inflammation and highly vascular granulation tissue persist after thorough deep scaling, the gingival tissue may require curettement under local anesthesia. The instrument blade is directed toward the soft tissues, and vertical and circumferential sweeping strokes are made in an attempt to remove all of the epithelial lining of the pocket as well as some of the inflamed tissue. To provide resistance to the instrument, one must use intrapapillary injections to make the tissue turgid and exert finger pressure on the outer surface of the gingiva to support the tissue (Fig. 6-23). Just a few strokes will usually suffice. The tissue is then pressed firmly against the tooth using a hot water–soaked gauze pad for close adaptation of the gingiva to tooth. No periodontal dressing is required, and usually little or no postoperative discomfort is encountered.

Ultrasonic instruments can be used in a similar manner. The instrument blade should be sharpened to provide a cutting edge. The ultrasonic vibrations of the instrument in contact with the gingiva will produce local coagulation of the inner lining, which is then easily removed.

The recent findings of bacterial invasion of the soft tissue wall of the pocket in both juvenile periodontitis and adult disease may provide a rationale for use of soft tissue curettage beyond that already suggested.

Operator, patient positions, and instrument choice

Two general approaches of the operator to the patient are described below and are illustrated in the following atlas. In the first approach, the patient is seated with the back and head at approximately a 45-degree angle to the floor. The operator works from the 7 to 12 o'-clock positions, depending on the area to be scaled. The patient's head is at approximately the level of the operator's elbows or slightly above. All diagrams for this approach are on the left side of the two-page demonstration of each technique. The second approach is one in which the patient is lying nearly horizontal and the operator works from behind the head in positions ranging from 10 to 12 o'clock.

The area being scaled is noted in the sectional arch drawing at the bottom of the page. The tooth representative of instrumentation for the segment is marked with an X. The instrument choice diagrams at the bottom of each page show each surface and line angle of the tooth divided into shallow and deep pockets as portions nearer and further from the anatomic tooth outline, respectively. Orientation of the tooth is facilitated by M (mesial), F (facial), D (distal), and L (lingual) designations.

Instruments are designated as follows: 4R, 4L, 2R, and 2L are McCall curettes; GR1 to GR14 are Gracey curettes; GF3 is the Goldman-Fox curette; and HF3, HF5, HF7, and HF11 are Hirschfeld files.

The direction of the stroke is given by the arrow adjacent to the instrument designation. Multiple arrows indicate that more than one direction is possible and frequently desirable. Note that some instruments are useful in shallow but not deep pockets. Generally, instruments for deep pockets are also equally effective in shallower pockets.

In the anterior segments, some instruments are used on the mesial half of a tooth, and their mates are used on the distal half. A vertical line on the facial or lingual surface will indicate this separation of use.

In the most posterior segments, instrument choice is the same for the two patient positions, thus, only one usage diagram will appear.

References

Chaiken, B.S., et al. Subgingival curettage. J. Periodontol. 25:340, 1954.

Friskopp, J., et al. A comparative, scanning electron microscopic study of supragingival and subgingival calculus. J. Periodontol. 51:553, 1980.

Hirschfeld, L., et al. Subgingival curettage in periodontal treatment. J. Am. Dent. Assoc. 44:301, 1952.

Maxillary right posteriors, buccal aspect.

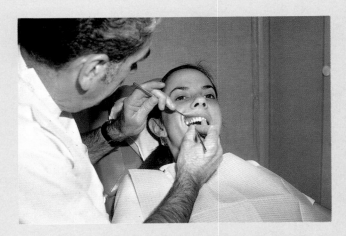

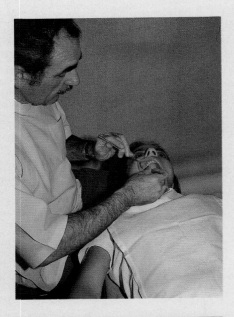

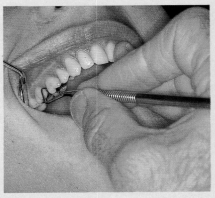

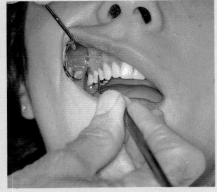

F

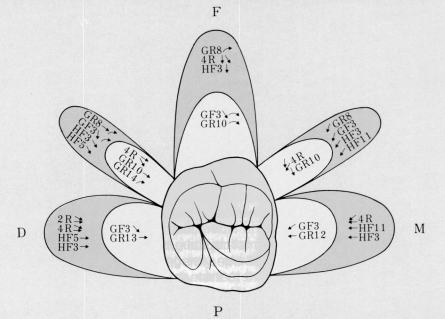

GR8
4R
HF3

GR8
GF3
HF3
HF5

4R
GR10
GR14

GF3
GR10

GR8
GF3
HF3
HF11

4R
GR10

D

2R
4R
HF5
HF3

GF3
GR13

GF3
GR12

4R
HF11
HF3

M

P

Maxillary right posteriors, palatal aspect.

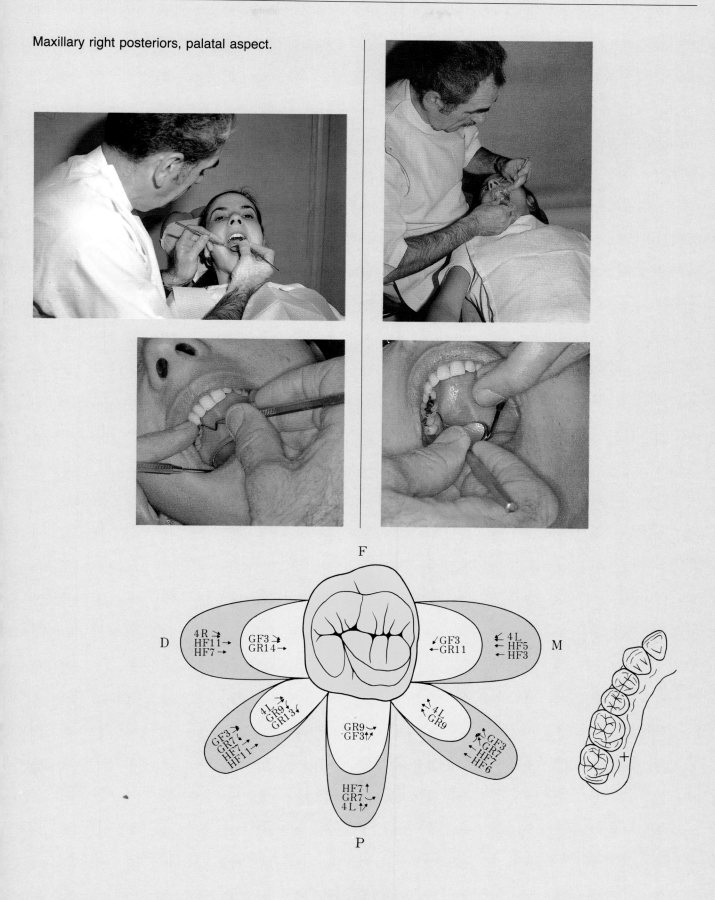

Maxillary left posteriors, buccal aspect.

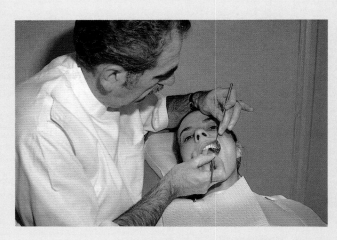

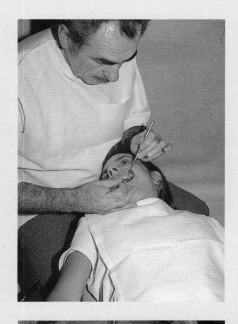

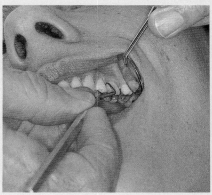

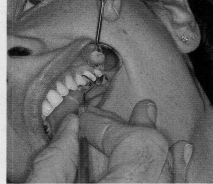

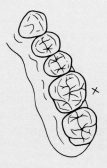

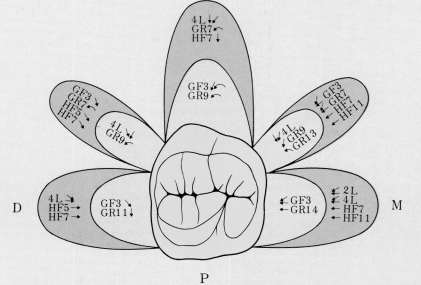

F

4L
GR7
HF7

GF3
GR9

GF3
GR7
HF5
HF7

GF3
GR7
HF7
HF11

4L
GR9

4L
GR9
GR13

D

4L
HF5
HF7

GF3
GR11

GF3
GR14

2L
4L
HF7
HF11

M

P

Maxillary left posteriors, palatal aspect.

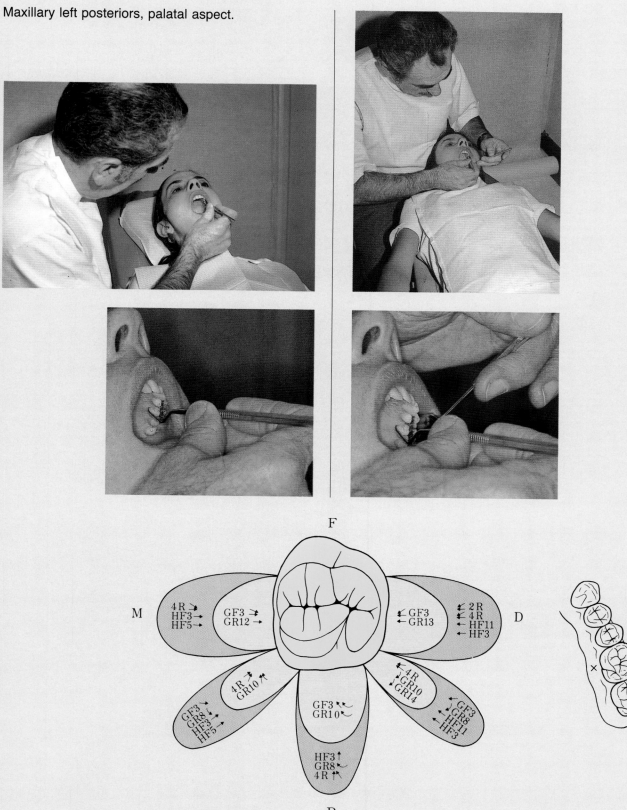

F

M   D

4R
HF3
HF5

GF3
GR12

GF3
GR13

2R
4R
HF11
HF3

4R
GR10

4R
GR10
GR14

GF3
GR8
HF3
HF5

GF3
GR8
HF11
HF3

GF3
GR10

HF3
GR8
4R

P

Root Scaling and Planing Techniques

Maxillary anteriors, palatal aspect.

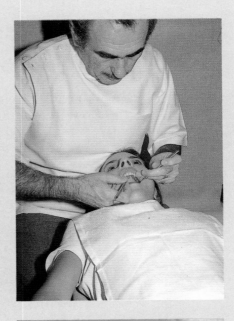

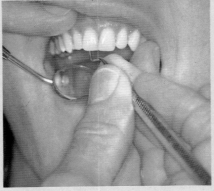

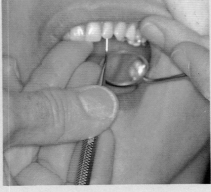

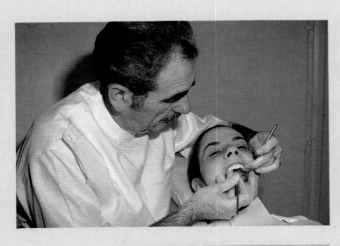

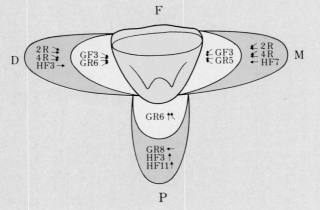

F

D 2R GF3 GF3 2R M
4R GR6 GR5 4R
HF3 HF7

GR6

GR8
HF3
HF11

P

Maxillary anteriors, labial aspect.

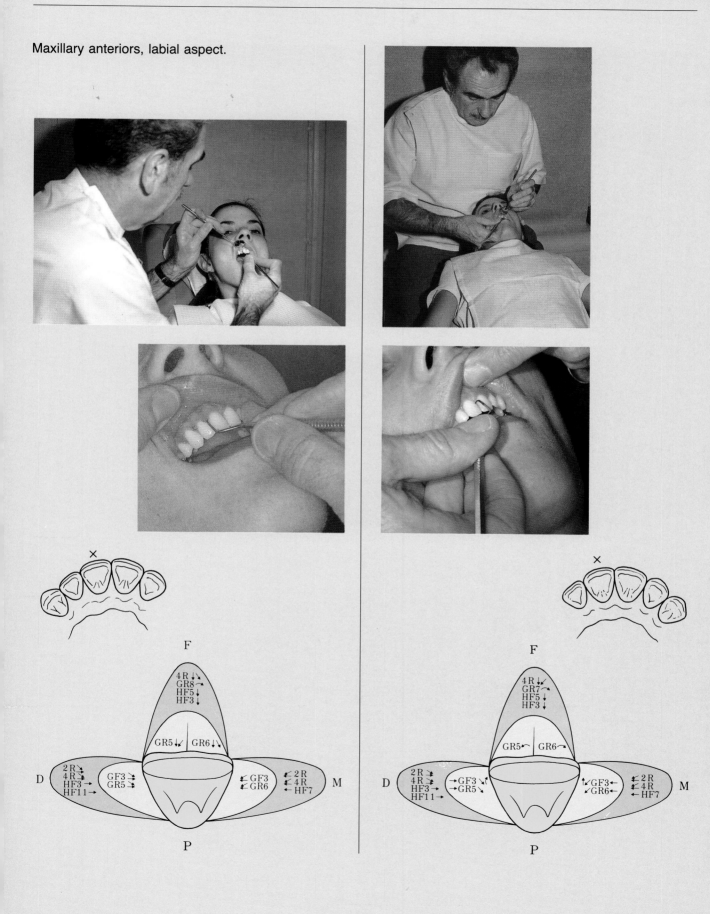

Root Scaling and Planing Techniques

Mandibular right posteriors, buccal aspect.

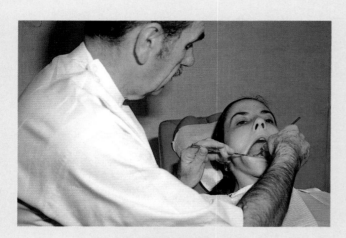

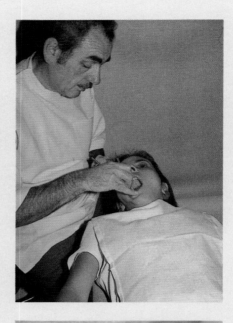

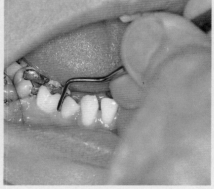

L

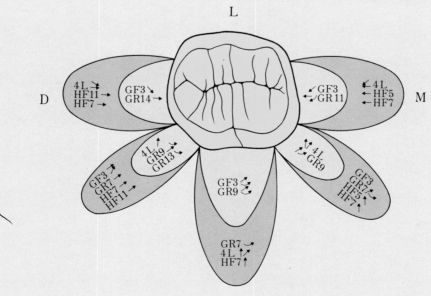

F

Mandibular right posteriors, lingual aspect.

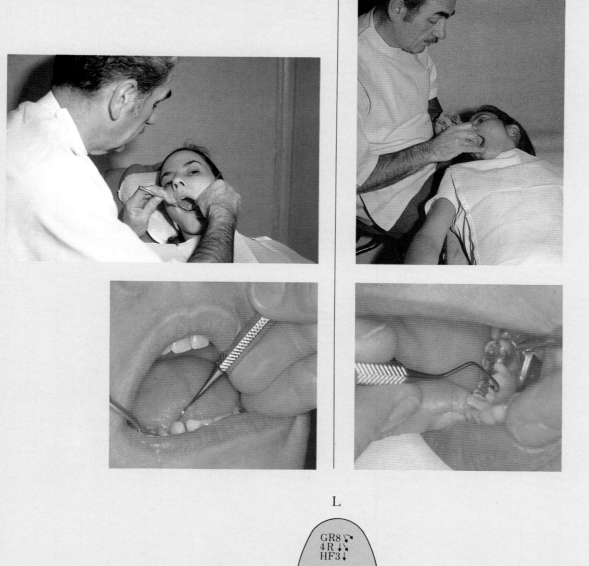

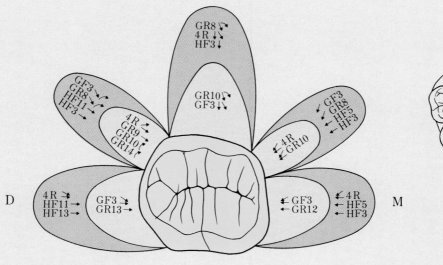

Root Scaling and Planing Techniques

Mandibular left posteriors, buccal aspect.

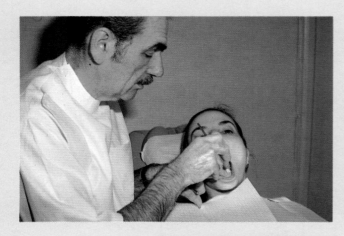

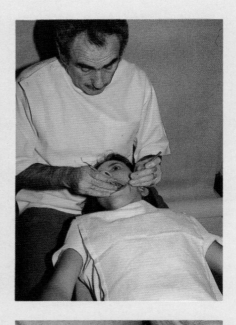

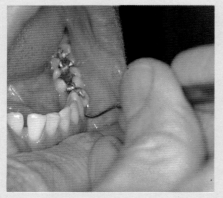

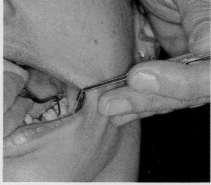

L

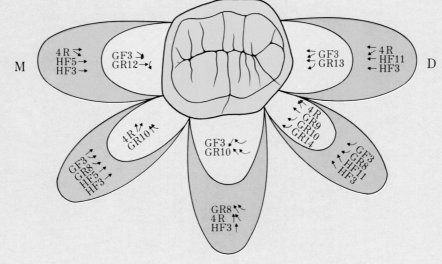

M

4R
HF5
HF3

GF3
GR12

GF3
GR13

4R
HF11
HF3

D

4R
GR10

4R
GR9
GR10
GR14

GF3
GR8
HF5
HF3

GF3
GR10

GF3
GR8
HF11
HF3

GR8
4R
HF3

F

Mandibular left posteriors, lingual aspect.

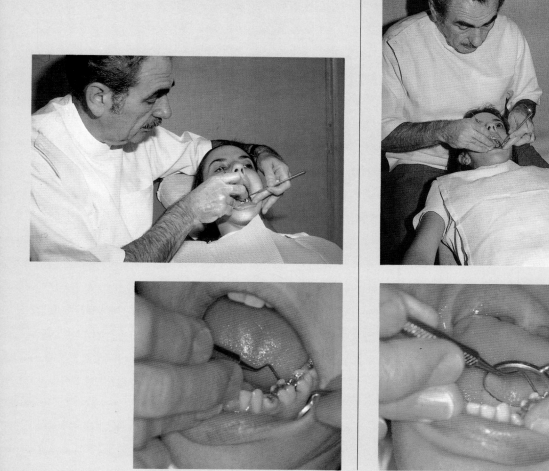

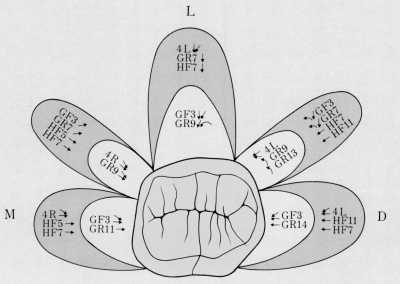

L

4 L ↓
GR7 ↓
HF7 ↓

GF3 ↓
GR9 ↓

GF3 ↙
GR7 ↙
HF7 ↓
HF11 ↓

GF3 ↘
GR7 ↘
HF5 →
HF7 →

4 R ↘
GR9 ↘

4 L ↙
GR9
GR13

M

4 R →
HF5 →
HF7 →

GF3 ↘
GR11 →

GF3 ↙
GR14 ←

4 L ↖
HF11 ←
HF7 ←

D

F

Root Scaling and Planing Techniques

Mandibular anteriors, lingual aspect.

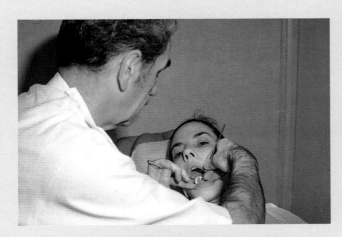

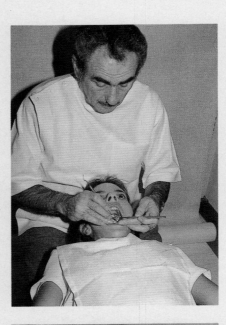

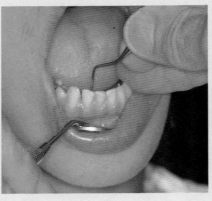

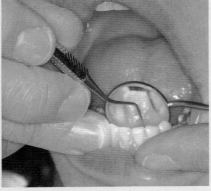

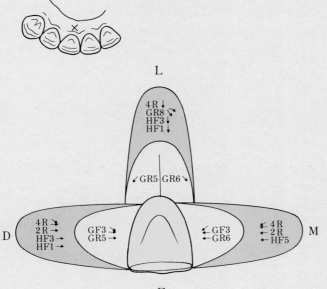

L

4 R ↓
GR8 ↘
HF3 ↓
HF1 ↓

↙GR5 GR6↘

D   4 R ↘   ↙GF3   ←GF3   ←4 R   M
     2 R →   GF3 GR5→   ←GR6   ←2 R
     HF3 →   GR5   ←GR6   ←HF5
     HF1 →

F

L

4 R ↘
GR7 ↘
HF7 ↓
HF11 ↓

↙GR5 GR6↘

D   4 L ↘   ↙GF3   ↙GF3   ←4 L   M
     2 L →   GF3 GR5→   ←GR6   ←2 L
     HF7 →   GR5   ←GR6   ←HF7
     HF5 →   ←HF11

F

Mandibular anteriors, labial aspect.

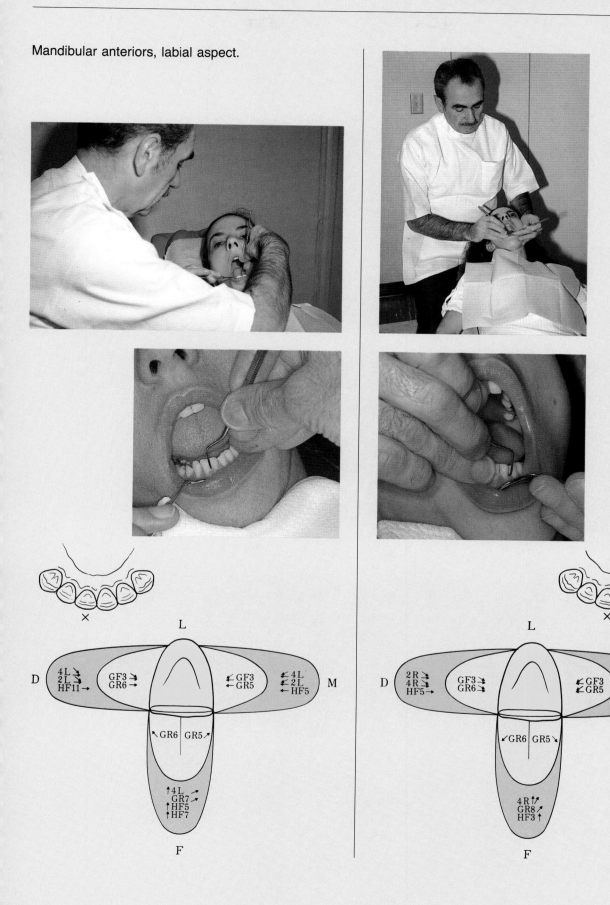

Chapter 7

Areas of Difficulty

The quantity and configuration of calculus seem to be related to the individual's tissue reactivity and the pathologic process. For example, in recurrent necrotizing gingivitis, spurlike projections of subgingival calculus limited to the proximal surfaces are almost pathognomonic for the disease (Fig. 7-1). The tenacity and hardness of calculus also seem to be associated with racial strains. These characteristics may reflect dietary or dental hygiene customs. Possibly heredity may determine such factors of tissue reactivity as vascular permeability or gingival fluid composition. I have had clinical experience with a group of Eastern European patients who form copious amounts of subgingival calculus associated with highly proliferative, inflammatory gingival responses. Poor oral hygiene was almost universally found. Calculus deposits in these individuals were spurlike and heavy but were relatively easily removed (Fig. 7-2). By contrast, many of my Chinese patients exhibited modest gingival inflammation with heavy spur or platelike calculus that was extremely tenacious. Though these and similar observations can be classified only as impressions, they are consistent enough to suggest the further investigation of the interrelation of ethnic groups and disease characteristics.

Amount and tenacity of subgingival calculus

The amount and tenacity of subgingival calculus, as well as the strength and nature of its bond to the root surface, may complicate scaling (Figs. 7-3a to c). In addition, there are instances during deep scaling and root planing procedures in which special attention is required because of the difficulty in access associated with dental anatomy and pocket configuration.

The tenacity of attachment can be gauged at examination by the attempt to remove some readily available deposit. Should the calculus be extremely tenacious, the operator should consider the relative merits of closed scaling with subgingival instruments, the use of the ultrasonic scaler, or open scaling of the roots after laying surgical flaps. If a closed procedure is to be used, heavy curettes and hand or ultrasonic scalers, which require greater tissue displacement dur-

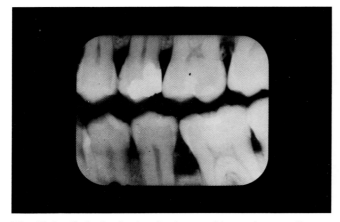

Fig. 7-1 Subgingival calculus and bone loss patterns characteristic of subacute necrotizing gingivitis of long standing. Bone loss is limited to the proximal surfaces, and calculus is spurred.

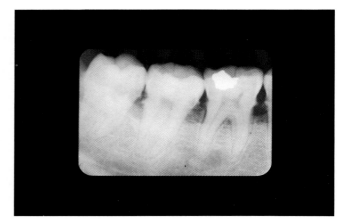

Fig. 7-2 Heavy subgingival calculus in a periodontitis case of an Eastern European ethnic subgroup.

Figs. 7-3a to c Variations in subgingival calculus form.

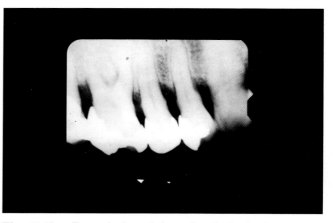

Fig. 7-3a Heavy deposits on adjacent anterior teeth, which are so heavy as to mechanically cause interdental soft tissue crater.

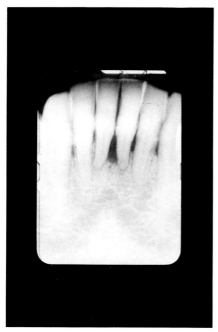

Fig. 7-3b Rounded nodules of subgingival calculus caused by repeated inadequate attempts at removal of calculus over many years.

Fig. 7-3c Thin, platelike calculus barely visible on the radiograph. There was no clinical gingival inflammation evident. Smoother calculus is evident on tooth 17.

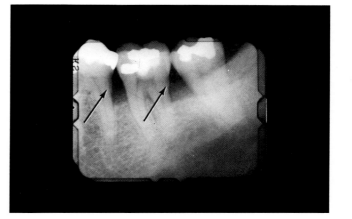

ing scaling, are advisable. Local anesthesia for pain control would also be advisable. A reasonable sequence of instrumentation for heavy tenacious deposits would be the careful subgingival use of heavy curettes, or ultrasonic scalers, followed by fine curettes, hoes, and files. Files can be used to crush deposits on difficult to reach surfaces also. Fine curettes will usually successfully complete the process.

Thin, smooth subgingival calculus

Though rare, the presence of thin, relatively smooth subgingival calculus poses a completely different problem. The tactile sense of the operator is put to a severe test since the differential between surface hardness and surface roughness rather than contour is the determinant of the presence of subgingival deposit (see Fig. 7-3c). Once chipping strokes remove some deposit, the differential between the calculus and cementum becomes more obvious, and calculus detection is facilitated. Fortunately, most calculus deposits are readily dislodged with some effort, although at best, complete calculus removal is very difficult.

Pocket locations

There are a number of pocket locations in which tooth anatomy complicates access to the calculus. Among these are *(1)* deep pockets on molars, *(2)* bifurcation and trifurcation involvements, *(3)* pockets on the line angles of almost all teeth, *(4)* direct palatal or facial pockets and pockets on narrow roots, and *(5)* narrow interradicular spaces.

Deep pockets on molars

Deep pockets on posterior teeth of more than 8 mm usually fall into a category wherein complete root debridement is extremely difficult. In such instances, surgical intervention should be entertained as a primary treatment modality. If there are compelling reasons, such as extremely advanced generalized disease, advanced age, or medical or psychologic reasons to contraindicate surgery, deep scaling alone can be attempted. For scaling of deep proximal pockets in posterior areas, hoes, files, and general utility curettes are most effective. Since shank-to-blade angles are greater in the Gracey curettes, they are less desirable in this circumstance than the McCall 4R or 4L or Goldman-Fox 3 curettes. Gracey curettes are useful in deep but wide proximal pockets into which the entire length of the blade can reach to the depth of the pocket. The instrumentation sequence would be the use of the hoe and file, followed by the curettes and files again. Testing very deep pockets for residual deposits may require using a periodontal probe to reach the most apical portions.

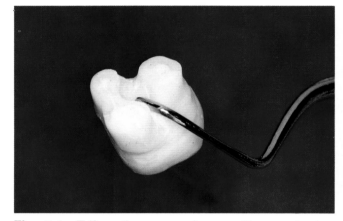

Fig. 7-4 Trifurcation area of a maxillary molar as viewed from the root apex. Roots were sectioned to provide view. Note extent of area as well as internal root contours that would be inaccessible to typical curette blade.

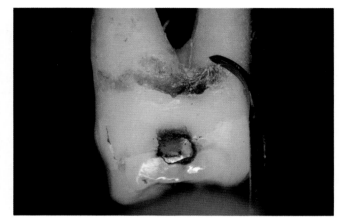

Fig. 7-5a Distobuccal root, distal surface scaling.

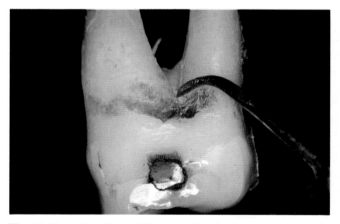

Fig. 7-5b Rotation of the curette tip toward the tooth makes access to the groove area possible.

Fig. 7-5c Curette tip within the radicular groove of a premolar.

Bifurcation and trifurcation involvements

Bifurcation and trifurcation involvements are almost impossible to scale completely. When one considers the anatomy of tooth furcation, it is obvious that few, if any, instruments will effectively negotiate all the root contours, especially on their internal surfaces (Fig. 7-4). Curettes are the most effective instrument type. Because of the angled blade, Gracey instruments present a narrower profile when viewed from the tip of the blade and are more effective in entering narrow furcations. It is best to complete scaling of the furcation with a given instrument and then return to the same area with another

Figs. 7-6a to d   Sequence of scaling a line angle.

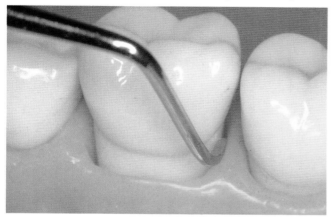

Fig. 7-6a   McCall 4R positioned on distal surface.

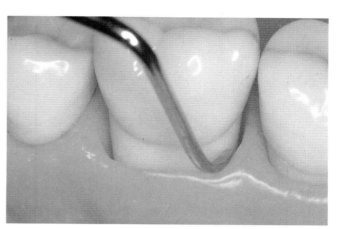

Fig. 7-6b   Distal of line angle.

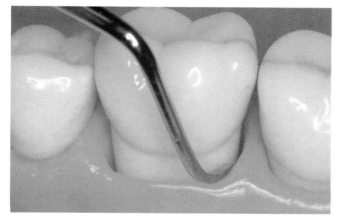

Fig. 7-6c   On line angle by changing position of rest.

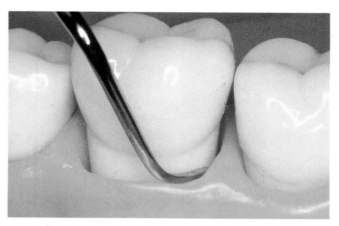

Fig. 7-6d   On lingual portion of line angle.

type of curette. Where accessible, line angles and internal surfaces are scaled with files as well. Grooves in the furcations are scaled with the tips of curettes (Figs. 7-5a to c).

Pockets on line angles of teeth

Line angles of teeth, especially the posterior teeth, present some difficulty in scaling. For premolars and molars, the line angles are reached by placing a general utility instrument such as the McCall 4R or 4L on the proximal surface and scaling with vertical strokes.

Figs. 7-7a to c Alternate sequence of scaling a line angle.

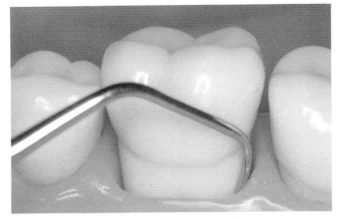

Fig. 7-7a Gracey 14 placed vertically for horizontal stroke from distal surface.

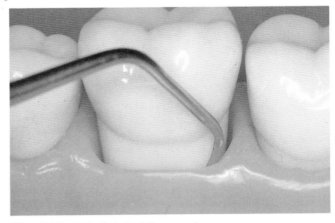

Fig. 7-7b At distal of line angle.

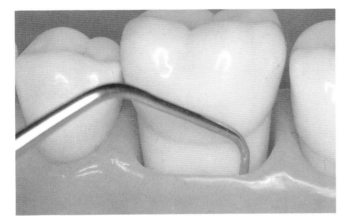

Fig. 7-7c Around to facial of line angle.

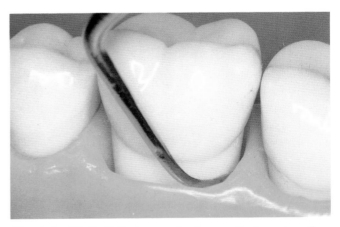

Fig. 7-8 McCall 4L (wrong instrument) placed on line angle with moderate pocket penetration but correct blade angle.

Then the finger rest is changed slightly so that the instrument can be placed on or near the line angle and that area scaled. The finger rest is again changed so that the blade can scale the line angle (Figs. 7-6a to d). Following this step, the area is scaled with diagonal or horizontal strokes, the instrument stroke extending from proximal to facial or lingual surfaces. The Gracey 7/8 and 13/14 curettes, with the blade pointing apically and using a horizontal stroke from proximal to lateral surfaces, will plane away all the remaining calculus (Figs. 7-7a to c). Should it be impossible to reach the line angle as described, the mate of the McCall instrument can be used essentially backward (Fig. 7-8). A vertical or angled stroke is used. Files are

Figs. 7-9a and b   Hirschfeld file 11.

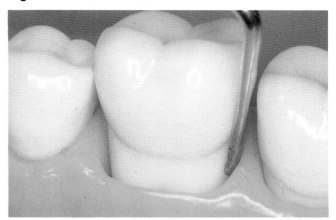 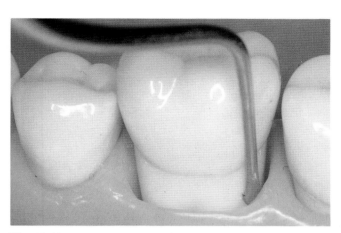

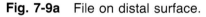

Fig. 7-9a   File on distal surface.

Fig. 7-9b   File on line angle.

also very useful on line angles, using care to overlap instrument strokes (Figs. 7-9a and b).

Palatal or facial pockets and pockets on narrow roots

Deep palatal or facial pockets and pockets on narrow-rooted teeth are best negotiated by use of the file. First, the pocket is expanded by entering the pocket with the instrument shank at an angle away from the long axis of the tooth. Then a more parallel position of the shank is assumed to engage the file blades for calculus removal. The surface is rescaled with a Gracey curette (7/8 or 13/14), with the blade placed parallel to the long axis of the tooth for greatest penetration using diagonal or circumferential strokes. Variations in the angulation and longitudinal curvature of portions of the root are compensated for by changing the angle of the blade. The operator must be ever aware of the lateral limits of the pocket to reduce damage to healthy attachment.

Narrow interradicular spaces

Narrow interradicular or interdental spaces are treated with a combination of push and pull strokes. The narrower the space, the greater dependence on push strokes. Instruments that have narrowed blades because of repeated sharpening are very useful.

Drifted and mesially inclined teeth

Teeth that have drifted and are mesially inclined are difficult to curette because of the altered relationship of the root surfaces. The mesial surfaces are best curetted with curettes that have the flat of the blade almost in a line with the long axis of the handle, such as the Goldman-Fox 3 or McCall 13/14. Other instruments normally used for mesial surfaces would be encumbered by the abnormal position of the crown.

References

Bower, R.C., et al. Furcation morphology relative to periodontal treatment: Furcation entrance architecture. J. Periodontol. 50:23, 1979.
Bower, R.C., et al. Furcation morphology relative to periodontal treatment: Furcation root surface anatomy. J. Periodontol. 50:366, 1979.

Chapter 8

Pain Control

The prospect of painful dental therapy in the psychologically charged oral cavity is at best unpleasant and at worst a deterrent to proper dental care. The unnecessary infliction of pain during deep scaling and root planing procedures reflects the indifference of the operator to the patient's comfort. Without anesthesia, only modest discomfort is sustained by most patients, even when deep periodontal pockets are scaled, providing that care is used during instrumentation. It is essential that practitioners school themselves in these simple methods, since periodontal patients are subject to repeated sectional arch deep scalings during both active treatment and single-session full dentition scalings during maintenance.

Pain sustained during deep scaling procedures is due either to injury to the gingiva or to instrument contact with exposed sensitive dentin.

Injury to the gingiva and the pocket wall soft tissues is usually due to *(1)* forceful entry into pockets, *(2)* careless choice of instrument, *(3)* overly vigorous exploratory strokes in either an apical or lateral direction, and *(4)* poor instrument control.

Simple techniques already described will help reduce pain. To reinforce a constant awareness and attention to patient comfort, I will briefly review some of these constraints:

1. Entry into pockets with unretracted, tightly adapted gingiva is accomplished by angling the instrument so that the flat of the blade is almost parallel to the root surface. The entry profile of the blade is thus reduced. Entry is begun at or near the tip of the blade, reducing gingival distention and pain (see Fig. 6-12). Files are angled away from the root surface to reduce their profile (see Fig. 6-13).
2. Exploratory and tactile strokes are made with a very gentle instrument grasp. The instrument should be held with only as much pressure as to prevent its slipping from the fingers when it is manipulated. With such a light grasp the resilience of the epithelial attachment and the rough surface of calculus are readily discerned.
3. Instruments must be chosen based on pocket and root size. Long-bladed instruments are useful only for wide-mouthed pockets or when they are used for diagonal or circumferential strokes. The narrow roots of anterior teeth and molars may require the

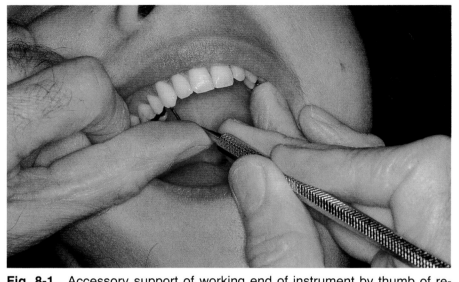

Fig. 8-1 Accessory support of working end of instrument by thumb of retracting hand reduces instrument slippage.

use of files or curettes in very short, well-controlled, diagonal or horizontal strokes.
4. Complete control of the instrument is mandatory. The working grasp must be firm and the strokes kept short. Repeated strokes in an area should duplicate one another in their apical movement so that the soft tissue remains undamaged. Accessory control may be obtained by supporting the shank of the instrument with the index finger or thumb of the nonworking hand (Fig. 8-1).

As standard procedure for all deep scaling, the use of topical anesthesia is advisable. Solutions containing 20% ethyl aminobenzoate (benzocaine) in polyglycols or ointments such as 5% lidocaine produce a mild surface anesthesia for the soft tissue. The delivery of the solution to the pocket can be made by direct application with cotton pledget or with the scaling instruments. The use of blunt-needled irrigating syringes to carry the topical anesthetics subgingivally produces better anesthesia than surface application. It is necessary to warm the thick ointment-based anesthetics to express them from the syringes.

Since approximately 30% of all teeth have a deficiency of cervical cementum, one would expect to find a wide incidence of sensitive cervical dentin. In cases of recurrent necrotizing gingivitis, the root surfaces adjacent to the interdental craters frequently exhibit root sensitivity. Most probably, the bacterial plaque accumulations in the protected environment of the gingival crater decalcifies the root surface, exposing the dentin. Root sensitivity may also develop on root surfaces subject to numerous scalings, which may have removed the cementum.

To control pain resulting from cervical dentinal exposure, one must keep the instrument within the pocket, limiting the number of entries and exits that might allow contact with the cervical dentin. Patient responses to pain should be observed, and the area of sensitivity should be studiously avoided. The patient can assist by identifying the pain as of tooth or soft tissue origin, thus indicating the pain control technique required.

Under those circumstances where tooth sensitivity is generalized and extreme, local infiltration with nerve block anesthesia or nitrous oxide analgesia is indicated. Similarly, where localized abscess formation requires root scaling in a highly sensitive and inflamed area, local infiltration anesthesia some distance anterior and posterior to the infected site is indicated.

During regular maintenance visits, the objective is to scale the whole dentition in a single session. For patients with many sensitive teeth, nitrous oxide analgesia is superior to multiple injections required for infiltration anesthesia. The choice of anesthetic agent should be left to the patient, since each agent will represent another form of personal discomfort, which may or may not be acceptable.

Hypnosis, which can provide a modest level of analgesia, is a very helpful aid during maintenance visits. After the patient has been induced into a trance state at an initial visit, the subsequent inductions take a very short time. Though the level of local analgesia will vary depending on the inherent hypnotizability of the patient, a serious attempt to produce analgesia will usually result in some measure of success. Hypnosis techniques are easily learned and readily perfected. The patient is relaxed and develops the confidence so important to a wholesome patient-practitioner relationship.

Posttreatment pain is directly related to the level of trauma inflicted during deep scaling procedures. The operator who assiduously observes the precepts for soft tissue pain control will reap the reward of patient comfort.

Sensitivity of root surfaces to instrumentation or even tooth brushing can be controlled in most instances. Dentin surfaces exposed to bacterial plaque undergo surface decalcification and become sensitive. These surfaces, if kept plaque-free, will undergo spontaneous remineralization with normal exposure to saliva. Thus, if good plaque control is practiced using the brush or tooth picks, root sensitivity will diminish. Should the roots be so sensitive that the dentin surface is avoided during brushing, a variety of desensitizing agents may be used. Sodium fluoride in concentration of 4% can be burnished into the surface. Iontophoresis devices, usually batter powered, can drive the fluoride ion of aqueous fluoride solutions into the dentin. Should these methods fail, agents such as tricalcium phosphate, sodium nitrate, or glycerol can be burnished into the surface at regular intervals. The surface may also be covered with fluoride-containing cavity varnish, or may be covered after surface conditioning with one of the free-flowing, low-filler, composite bonding materials. The surface of the dentin below the composite will become insensitive, even when the composite covering is finally lost. Should all else fail, the use of a restoration, which obliterates the sensitive dentin by cavity preparation, may be indicated.

Chapter 9

Choice and Sequence of Treatment

Assessment and relationship of radiographic, pathologic, and clinical findings

Formulation of a treatment plan begins the moment that undistorted and well-processed radiographs are available to the practitioner. Before examination of the patient, the radiographs should be examined, with special notation made of a number of characteristics of the pattern of the case. These are:

I. Pattern of bone loss
    A. Horizontal (Fig. 9-1)
    B. Angular (Fig. 9-2)
    C. Generalized (Fig. 9-3)
    D. Localized (Fig. 9-4)
        1. Symmetric bone loss (Fig. 9-5)
        2. Assymetric bone loss
        3. Proximal, facial or lingual loss
        4. Jaw predisposition (Fig. 9-5)
II. Furcation involvements (Fig. 9-6)
III. Root proximity, including the roots of a single lower molar (Fig. 9-6)
IV. Calculus distribution, form, and amount (Fig. 9-7)
V. Previous and current caries activity (Fig. 9-8)

The overview of the radiographs will provide the operator with a sense of the pathologic condition of the dentition. The clinical examination should assume some diagnostic direction in addition to making a graphic rendition of pathologic conditions. Each succeeding bit of data should help to answer some of the questions inherent in proper diagnosis. What is the disease? How can this patient's disease be characterized? What casual relationship exists? What was the natural history of the disease in that patient, and what are the etiologic factors in their relative order of importance?

Are local etiologies related to local pathology? Are the same etiologic agents, such as plaque and calculus or poor dentistry, present in other areas of the dentition where no pathologic condition exists? Can we adequately eliminate or control etiologic factors to control the disease? What etiologic factors cannot be controlled, and just how important are these? What treatment modalities would be most successful? What level of esthetic requirement need be satisfied?

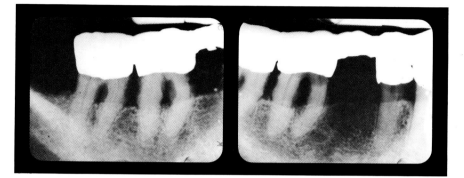

Fig. 9-1 Patterns of bone loss. Horizontal crestal bone loss simplifies treatment by deep scaling or excision surgery.

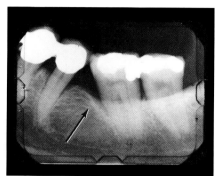

Fig. 9-2 Periodontitis with angular bone defects is associated primarily with wide interradicular bone septa and only secondarily with trauma from occlusion.

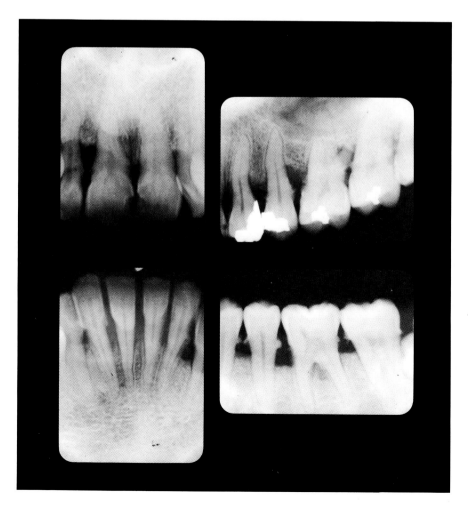

Fig. 9-3 Periodontitis affecting most or all of the teeth requires definitive treatment in all areas.

126

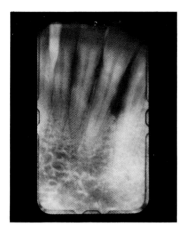

Fig. 9-4 Localized bone loss may be associated with a specific local cause, such as crowding.

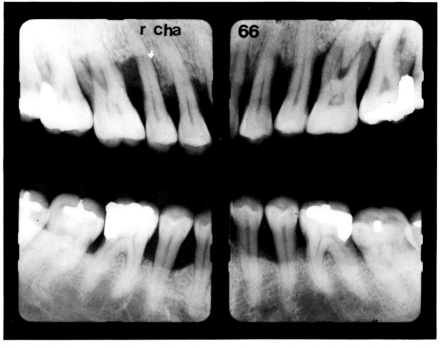

Fig. 9-5 Symmetric bone loss in an advanced periodontitis is the rule rather than the exception. The maxillary arch may exhibit greater destruction than the mandibular arch, as illustrated. The reverse is equally common.

Fig. 9-7 Calculus quantity and form: *(a)* no calculus in juvenile periodontitis, *(b)* spurlike calculus, *(c)* nodular calculus, *(d)* platelike calculus.

Fig. 9-6 Maxillary molar with trifurcation bone destruction. Entry into the trifurcation could be made from both the distal and facial surfaces of the tooth. The prognosis of the tooth is guarded. Note proximity of divergent distal root to adjacent second molar. Root amputation was indicated.

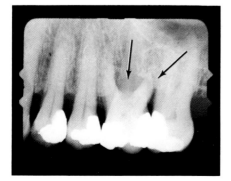

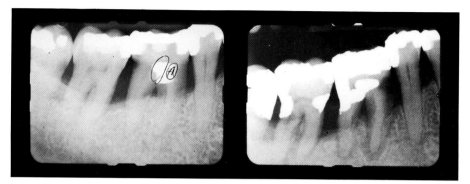

Fig. 9-8 Caries-susceptible dentition with extensive decay and pulp devitalization after root exposure by periodontal surgery. Resective surgery in such cases should be avoided.

As the recording of pocket depth, mobility, and gingival changes in a dentition progresses, the operator must constantly relate each observation with the radiographic overview and with the impression he or she has already developed concerning the nature of the case. The mind is never still during the routine of the examination. Observe and relate pathogenesis. If inflammation is present, define its nature, and relate it to the amount and form of calculus and plaque. Is there a geographic distribution for the inflammation, or is it localized? If it is localized, what is the status of the restorations? Is oral hygiene selectively poor? If the inflammation occurs in the anterior segments only, is the patient a mouth breather? Is the inflammation an inflammatory hyperplasia with severe bleeding on probing, gingival enlargement, and deep, red gingival color? Is the gingiva cyanotic and exhibiting little gingival enlargement and inflammation even though there is considerable pocket depth? Is the gingiva thick and pink, with the margins located high on the crowns? Are we dealing with a delayed passive eruption or an idiopathic fibromatosis? Is the gingiva generally red without much inflammatory enlargement? If so, is the patient an alcoholic?

These questions relate to inflammation only. However, a multitude of other such relationships must be established or denied. An examination directed in this manner will frequently provide information that is overlooked when examination procedure is done by rote or by checklist. The patient's medical and dental history, both of which should be very inclusive, must be reviewed and amplified by questions prompted by the radiographic and clinical findings as well as the projected therapies.

If a generalized horizontal bone loss was found on the radiographs, we might see a number of clusters of anatomic and clinical signs that could be associated with such a pathologic condition. For mature adults the clusters of signs could include:

1. Heavy spurlike subgingival calculus surrounding all teeth with generalized severe inflammatory hyperplasia. The pocket depth measurements would be greater than expected because of the gingival inflammatory enlargement. Severe bleeding would occur on probing. Very poor oral hygiene would be evident (see Fig. 9-3).
2. Moderately heavy subgingival calculus, moderate gingival edema, and unexpectedly moderate to severe gingival recession present about all surfaces of teeth. The teeth would be large in relation to the thin alveolar housing. Slight to moderate bleeding would occur on probing. Oral hygiene could be relatively good, with only small quantities of supragingival plaque present (Figs. 9-9a and b).
3. Cyanotic gingiva with no recession or gingival inflammatory enlargement and moderate amounts of subgingival calculus. Pocket depths are moderate to severe with less than expected bleeding on probing. Oral hygiene could be relatively good with slight amounts of plaque and supragingival calculus (Figs. 9-10a and b).

In an aged adult, uniform bone loss is frequently associated with generalized gingival recession and rather thin alveolar processes. The gingiva could exhibit slight to moderate inflammation (Fig. 9-11). The gingiva would appear receded around all the teeth, giving the appearance of a surgically treated case.

Given the simple radiographic finding of horizontal bone loss, the patient could manifest periodontal disease in a variety of clinical forms. As a consequence, each type would react somewhat differently to deep scaling and root planing and would therefore have different surgical requirements. Each of these variations is a response to what would seem to be the same primary etiologic factors—plaque and calculus.

These overall variations of the pathologic response obviously reside within the individual and represent an interplay between systemically determined responses and the influence of local modifying conditions. The extremes of clinically evident tissue responses to irritants are a general proliferative inflammatory response as opposed to an essentially noninflammatory or atrophic response. The consistently good, immediate, and long-term successes using definitive deep scaling result from treatment of the clinically inflamed cases. A diagnosis of inflamed or noninflamed case type during examinations will be a factor in determining both the periodontal treatment plan and the ultimate prognosis of the dentition.

Distribution of teeth affected

The distribution of teeth affected by periodontal destruction will also help define the diagnosis. When, in a young patient, only the anterior teeth and first molars have deep pockets, with little gingival inflammation, a diagnosis of juvenile periodontitis (periodontosis) should be considered. Arc-like bony defects in the radiographs extending

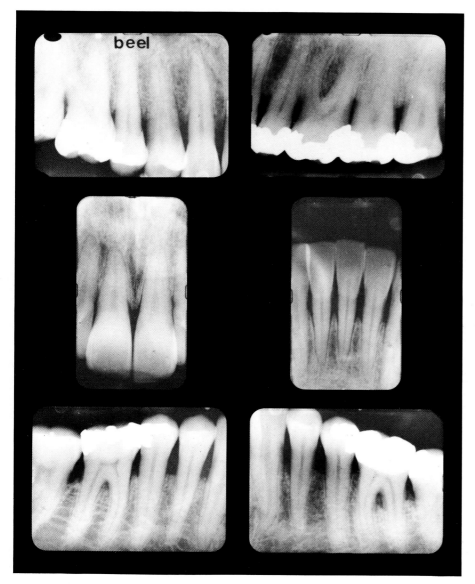

Figs. 9-9a and b Generalized horizontal loss with gingival recession resulting from local irritational factors in conjunction with oversized teeth in narrow alveolar processes.

Fig. 9-9a Radiographic changes.

Fig. 9-9b Clinical gingival recession and slight inflammation.

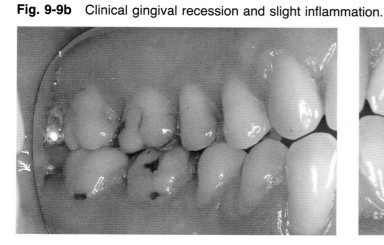
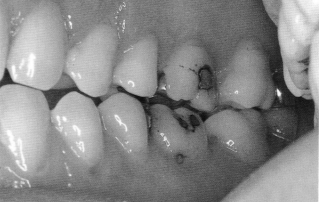

130

Figs. 9-10a and b Bone loss in a noninflammatory case with cyanotic gingiva.

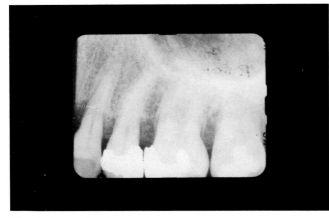

Fig. 9-10a Radiographic changes.

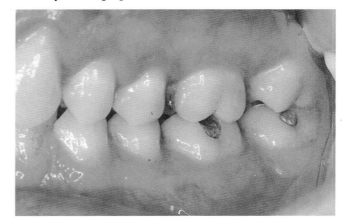

Fig. 9-10b Generalized gingival cyanosis in the absence of inflammatory hyperplasia.

Fig. 9-11 Man, aged 75, with extensive horizontal gingival and bony recession with clinically healthy gingiva.

from the mesial to distal surfaces of the first molars are almost pathognomonic for this disease. Similar patterns of bone loss and pocket depth in an adult should prompt a diagnosis of an arrested periodontosis. In these cases, the molar lesions are bilaterally symmetric. Since exact bilateral symmetry of disease implies a strong systemic influence in the disease process, the periodontosis group of conditions may be difficult to control by simple elimination of local etiologic factors (see Fig. 1-22). The patient should be so advised at diagnosis.

In general, chronic periodontitis is also usually bilaterally symmetric. The presence of pocket depth around a molar should prompt the examiner to carefully probe the contralateral molar for similar pockets. Frequently, a similar pathologic condition will be found. In early disease, the molars are usually the teeth affected. The premolars and anterior teeth become involved as the disease develops further. Most patients do not sustain more than moderate disease in some segments of the dentition. Thus, in many instances the therapy should be divided on the basis of severity of disease, pocket reduction surgery being required in some segments and deep scaling and root planing elsewhere. By noting the pattern of disease at diagnosis, the operator can better define the ultimate treatment plan.

Surfaces of teeth affected by periodontitis

The surfaces of individual teeth are variably affected by periodontal disease. In most instances, proximal surfaces are affected; frequently the facial and lingual surfaces remain normal. In patients who have only proximal pockets on approximating surfaces, it is essential to determine whether proximal gingival craters are present. The examiner should move the probe from the mesial to the distal surfaces of the approximating teeth at or near the depth of the pocket. In true cratering, no gingival tissue will be encountered. If the craters are of long standing, they frequently will be associated with heavy spurlike calculus. Then a diagnosis of subacute necrotizing gingivitis should be considered and substantiated by the patient's dental history. Usually a history of recurrent low-grade gingival tenderness and bleeding will be described, corroborating the diagnosis. Deep scaling will frequently produce regeneration and reattachment of the proximal gingiva. On the other hand, isolated molar interdental gingival craters with deep pockets and horizontal bone loss with a similar history are rarely responsive to deep scaling.

Periodontal pockets limited to closely approximating root surfaces of two adjacent teeth will respond poorly to definitive deep scaling. If tooth rotation or malalignment are the cause for the root proximity, tooth movement should be considered. Interdental bony craters are frequently found between the flared distobuccal root of the maxillary first and the mesial root of the second molar. Narrow interradicular distances in combination with a susceptibility to disease will often cause extensive bone loss about one or both of the approximating roots (Figs. 9-12a and b). Root amputation should be considered. Other areas where root proximity, in conjunction with a diathesis toward disease, will produce interdental bony crater are crowded lower anterior teeth, especially the lateral-canine area, and the interdental septa between rotated teeth. Orthodontic tooth movement should be considered in such cases since deep scaling alone may fail to control disease progress.

A deep proximal pocket on one surface of an individual tooth will usually require surgical treatment to attempt regeneration of attachment. For a single deep proximal pocket, a judgment concerning the influence of that deep pocket on the approximating root surface must be made. A marked destructive influence on the adjacent tooth sur-

Figs. 9-12a and b Interdental bony crater between teeth 14 and 15.

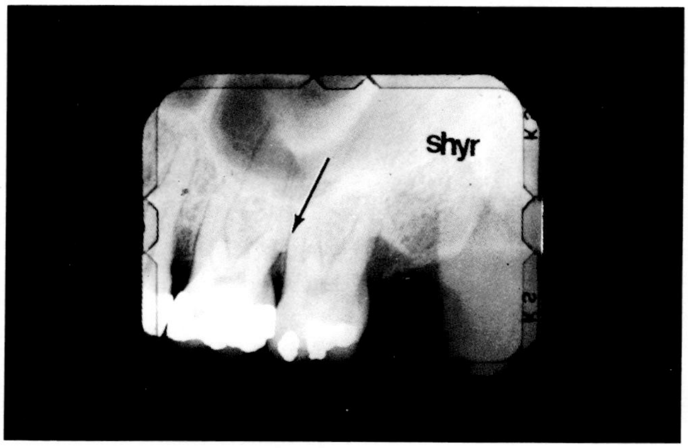

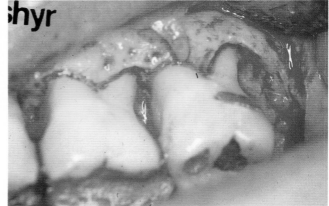

Fig. 9-12a Radiograph.

Fig. 9-12b During surgical procedure.

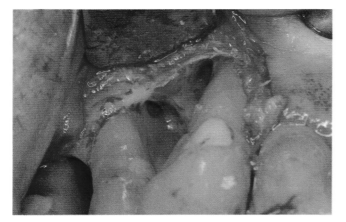

Fig. 9-13 Adjacent infrabony defects with residual bone midway on the interradicular septum are treated as separate infrabony lesions.

face would suggest extraction of the offending tooth. In wide interdental septas, equal destruction without bony cratering could lead to formation of two infrabony pockets. Surgical intervention to attempt reattachment is indicated (Fig. 9-13).

Furcation involvements

Careful examination for furcation involvements in all areas of inter-radicular radiolucency is mandatory. In addition, on multiple-rooted teeth, any pocket exceeding 5 mm should be further examined for furcation involvement. Curved periodontal probes or fine currettes should be used to attempt entry into the furcation. Incipient furcation involvements (Class I) are most amenable to definitive deep scaling. When instruments can penetrate well into the furcation (Class II or III involvements), calculus and plaque removal is usually incomplete. The deepest portion of the roof of the furcation is difficult to scale since access is limited by the anatomic configuration of the area. The internal surfaces of the involved roots are difficult to scale as well. Since extension of the lesion occurs at its lateral and apical borders, these teeth are usually classified as having questionable long-term prognoses. Any prosthetic treatment plan that includes a furcated tooth must therefore incorporate a contingency plan for tooth loss. The other possibility would be for the operator to consider eradication of the furcation involvement either by hemisection, root amputation, or tooth extraction before restoration.

Tooth mobility

Tooth mobility will depend on the interplay of such anatomic factors as root length, root circumference, tooth position, the ratio of extra and intraalveolar tooth lengths, and the forces of occlusion. The intensity and duration of the forces of occlusion during afunctional tooth contacts in conjunction with the individual periodontium's response to occlusal forces will determine tooth mobility. The radiographs indicate some of the anatomic factors; these must be correlated with pertinent clinical signs. Occlusal wear patterns are an invaluable guide to the examiner in determining the exact afunctional clenching and grinding movements made by the patient. The operator needs to observe the close interdigitation of opposing wear facets, insisting that the jaw movements be extended enough to include contact of all worn surfaces. Movement of the teeth, either intrusive or lateral, during centric and intercuspal contact and through the full range of used excursions of the mandible can be observed visually or by palpation, thus defining the location of occlusal overload. This degree of movement, induced by dynamic occlusion, usually reflects in the static mobility of the teeth, which is measured by gentle tapping of the tooth from side to side with the handles of two instruments.

Assessment of the forces producing mobility, the actual tooth mobility, and the ability of the operator to control the overload will determine the nature of treatment. If the remaining level of periodontal attachment has been only slightly compromised and occlusal overload is the cause for the tooth hypermobility, reduction of forces will lessen the hypermobility. This reversible circumstance is known as *primary occlusal trauma.* Should the loss of periodontal support be

so great that even the small functional occlusal forces during masti-
cation and swallowing cause hypermobility, the irreversible hypermobility is deemed caused only secondarily by occlusal trauma. The
judgment implies that some form of splinting is required to provide
additional support for the weakened tooth. Should the splints be full-
coverage restorations, surgical pocket reduction to establish stable
gingival margins would be indicated rather than deep scaling. Thus,
at examination, the observations concerning the factors of occlusion
and the resultant tooth mobility determine the use of deep scaling in
the treatment plan.

Relating graphic charting and radiographic findings

The charting of pocket depth and mobility must now be checked for
any possible overlooked pathologic condition by reviewing the radiographs and correlating the findings. Specifically, one should recon-
cile the following:

1. Pocket depth measurements and bone loss.
2. Mobility recordings and the level of alveolar bone.
3. Root size, shape, length and mobility. The mobility should be ex-
   plained on the basis of anatomy and trauma. Generalized mobility
   may represent the patient's response rather than local trauma.
4. Radiolucency in bifurcation and trifurcations and clinical recordings of such involvements.
5. The pattern of bone loss and pocket depth and expected patterns
   for periodontosis or periodontitis. If loss is present only on the
   distal surface of second molars, review the history for extraction
   of impacted third molars, a nonperiodontal cause.
6. The presence of pockets deeper than would be expected from
   bone levels, suggesting inflammatory or idiopathic hyperplasia of
   the gingiva or a delayed passive eruption of the teeth.
7. The form, quantity, and location of subgingival calculus and the
   type and severity of periodontal pathologic conditions present.

The corrected charting, radiographs, and the obvious local and
possible systemic causes must now be evaluated to determine the
level of controllability of the disease that can be expected by local
therapy. The less well-defined the relationships between local etiology and disease, the greater the possibility for failure of treatment in
the long term. The fewer the unknown causes and the less the systemic influence, the more predictable the results of therapy.

Formulation of a treatment plan

At this point, a periodontal treatment plan should be formulated. Using the guidelines for predictable success in the use of definitive deep scaling, the segments of the dentition falling within those boundaries should be treated with deep scaling.

Those segments requiring surgery should follow an orderly sequence. Angular bony defects that are narrow and deep and may, therefore, respond by bony regrowth are considered first. Since the reconstitution of the periodontium is the ideal result, surgical procedures to effect this result should be planned for early in treatment. Those bony defects that are not amenable to reattachment procedures or control by deep scaling should be subject to eradication surgery. Should a segment of the dentition require surgical treatment, logic forces us to consider surgical treatment of pockets in adjacent areas that might ordinarily be controlled by definitive deep scaling alone. The esthetics of the anterior portion of the dentition is of primary importance to many patients and will modify the treatment plan toward less excision surgery and more toward deep scaling and conservative flap procedures.

The order of periodontal therapy is usually as follows:

1. Prophylaxis and oral hygiene instruction
2. Definitive deep scaling and root planing, presurgical scaling, or all of these
3. Surgical treatment
4. Selective tooth grinding–orthodontic tooth movement
5. Execution of the prosthetic plan
6. Occlusal appliances to reduce afunctional overloading
7. Maintenance

The pattern is modified when any acute or painful symptoms are present. Acute abscesses or an acute necrotizing gingivitis is treated by deep scaling or debridement and antibacterial therapy, respectively. Severely mobile, painful teeth are selectively ground to reduce overloading. Since slight repositioning of the teeth will occur as inflammation subsides, only gross reductions of occlusal interferences should be carried out during the early stages of treatment.

Where tooth movement will enhance the possibility of successful surgical management of a lesion, the orthodontic movement is begun immediately after deep scaling. Examples are severely tipped teeth and teeth with wide proximal intrabony pockets where movement will eliminate or modify the bony defect and the subsequent surgical procedure.

The goals of deep scaling will determine the number of visits allocated to that form of therapy. Definitive scaling for hyperplastic inflammatory cases requires the greatest number of sessions, whereas a single presurgical scaling for a noninflammatory case might well be adequate. Oral hygiene instruction must be instituted early and should be reinforced throughout therapy until the home care is as near perfect as can be executed by the patient.

If teeth must be lost because of disease, or if the dentition is missing teeth that require replacement, the periodontal treatment plan is affected. When fixed prostheses are contemplated, the periodontal treatment plan should be directed toward disease control by surgical pocket eradication. At the termination of such periodontal treatment, the established gingival levels will be more stable than after definitive deep scaling, where some pocket depth might remain. With no such prosthetic requirement, cases with some residual pocket depth after definitive deep scaling may be maintained for many years.

Actual surgical techniques, prosthetic requirements, and methods for occlusal adjustment are beyond the province of this text and are explored completely in other texts in this series.

References

Caton, J.G., et al. The attachment between tooth and gingival tissues after periodic root planing and soft tissue curettage. J. Periodontol. 50:462, 1979.

Nyman, S., et al. A longitudinal study of combined periodontal and prosthetic treatment of patients with advanced periodontal disease. J. Periodontol. 50:163, 1979.

Polson, A.M., et al. Interrelationship of inflammation and tooth mobility (trauma) in pathogenesis of periodontal disease. J. Clin. Periodontol. 7:351, 1980.

Ritchey, B., et al. The crests of the interdental alveolar septa. J. Periodontol. 24:75, 1953.

Chapter 10

Maintenance Phase

Active treatment should restore the health of the periodontium to the extent that periodic scalings will suffice to maintain the result. Maintenance of health in treated cases is an obligation of the practitioner and requires a combination of skills, which include efficient deep scaling technique, detection of exacerbations of destructive disease, observation of occlusal changes made apparent by increased tooth mobility, and assessment of the patient's oral hygiene effectiveness. Finding even the slightest pathologic change should alert the operator to the need for detection of cause and responsive alteration of treatment.

The recall visit should include the following observations and treatment:

1. Check effectiveness of oral hygiene, noting areas of ineffective plaque control.
2. Observe gingival inflammation by noting even slight color, contour, and bleeding changes. Test for suppuration by lightly pressing just below the gingival margins with a rounded instrument.
3. Check all suspicious areas for new or increased pocket depth.
4. Check changes in static tooth mobility by alternately tapping each tooth in a buccal then lingual direction and observing tooth movement during scaling. Test intrusive mobility by applying pressure to the individual teeth and observing tooth intrusion when the teeth occlude.
5. Scale and polish the teeth.
6. Adjust the occlusion to reduce any overloading.
7. Periodically recheck bone levels with new radiographs.
8. Reevaluate effectiveness of maintenance program, and recommend necessary additional treatment or changes in program.

The maintenance visit is usually spaced at a 4- to 6-month interval. In general, calculus accumulated over the short recall visit is light and the calculus is easily removed. Fortunately, the microflora reestablishes itself slowly, which makes it possible to stabilize the case for long posttreatment periods. Heavy calculus producers may require considerable deep scaling, especially if residual pockets are present. The presence of heavy calculus will make it most difficult to completely scale such a dentition in a single visit—the goal of successful active treatment. To reestablish proper control of such cases, additional surgical pocket reduction is indicated.

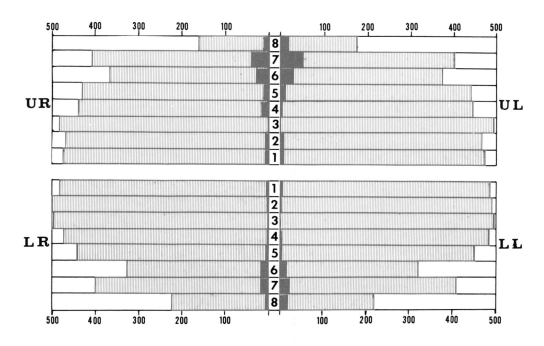

Fig. 10-1 Distribution of teeth lost *(solid area)* in relation to teeth present at initial examination in well-maintained group (83% of sample) during an average of 22 years. Note symmetric loss, primacy of molar tooth loss, and no loss of canines.

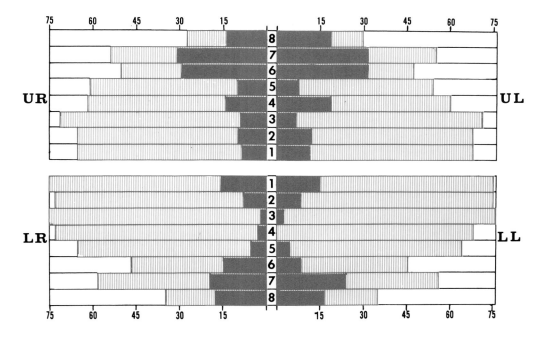

Fig. 10-2 Distribution of teeth lost in relation to teeth present at initial examination in downhill group (12% of sample). Note broader distribution of tooth loss, with minimal loss of mandibular canines and first premolars.

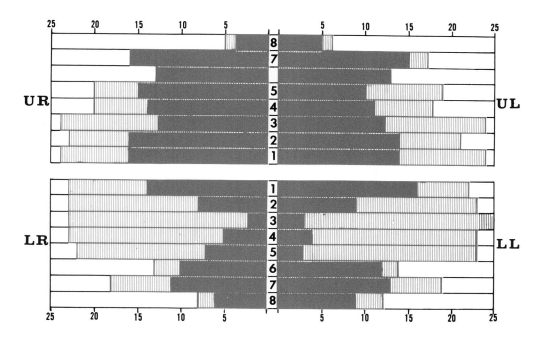

Fig. 10-3 Distribution of teeth lost in relation to teeth present at initial examination in extreme downhill group (4% of sample). Note relative resistance to loss of the mandibular canines and premolars.

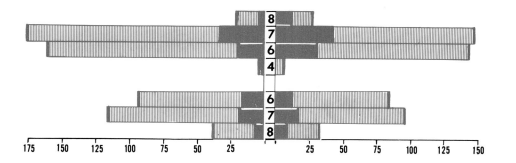

Fig. 10-4 Distribution of questionable teeth with furcation involvement, which were lost in relation to furcated teeth at the initial examination in the well-maintained group. Note only 19% were lost.

Long-term maintenance of most cases is possible if consistent recall is practiced. A study of tooth mortality in 600 patients during an average maintenance period of 22 years in my practice indicated the following:

1. Though the patients, on average, had similar severity of periodontal disease at the beginning of treatment, 83% of the patients lost fewer than four teeth during maintenance. Twelve percent lost between five and nine teeth, and 4% lost more than nine teeth. The reduction in pocket depth as a result of active treatment was similar. However, during the long period of maintenance, the well-maintained group (fewer than four teeth lost) exhibited a resistance to new periodontal lesions, so that the type of teeth lost closely reflected the distribution and severity of disease at examination (Fig. 10-1). Thus, molar teeth, which in general were most diseased, were the most frequently lost during maintenance. However, even in this group about 20% of the teeth lost had favorable prognoses at onset. The slow downhill group dentitions (four to nine teeth lost) exhibited advancing periodontal lesions of the originally affected teeth as well as a greater tendency toward tooth loss from new lesions (Fig. 10-2). Of the teeth lost, 43% originally were deemed to have good prognoses, approximately twice as high as in the well-maintained group. In the extreme downhill group (ten to 23 teeth lost), 46% of the teeth lost were originally designated as having good prognoses (Fig. 10-3).

Thus, the concept of individual response and resistance to the disease is inescapable. A simple course of treatment almost completely stabilized the disease in the well-maintained group, whereas similar treatment did not deter future loss in the downhill groups.

2. The presence of bifurcation and trifurcation involvements in 83% of the cases (well-maintained group) did not lead to tooth loss. In this group only 19% of all furcated teeth were lost (Fig. 10-4). Since few root amputations were done, many interradicular pockets persisted after treatment of these molar teeth. Since scaling of the root surfaces within the bifurcation area is almost always less than complete, it would seem that the rate of destruction was decreased significantly by removal of most, but probably not all, of the subgingival deposits in some cases. As with all chronic disease, periodontal disease exhibits periods of activity and periods of remission, both locally and for the dentition. The resistance to progress of the furcation lesions in the face of residual plaque should not be taken as license to do poor deep scaling. Rather, it indicates the level of resistance as well as the nature of the disease process in the majority of our patients. In the remaining 16% of the study population, approximately 75% of all furcated teeth were lost.

3. Pocket eradication is probably not the primary determinant for long-term maintenance. The downhill groups, incidentally, had proportionately more pocket eradication surgeries than the well-maintained group.

4. Gingival inflammation was a common finding at recall visits in many patients from all groups. This finding suggested that gingival

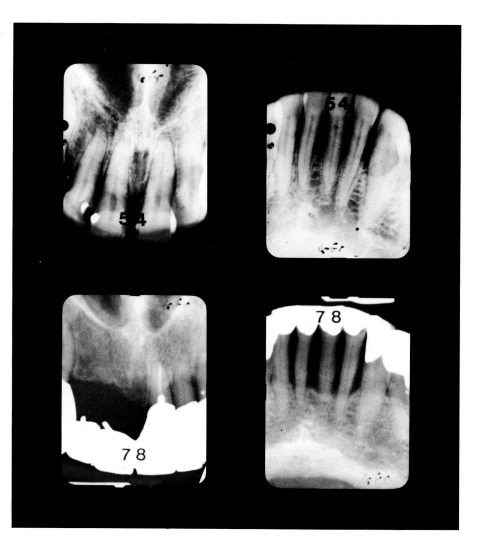

Fig. 10-5 Long-term treated case. 1954 radiographs of a case with noninflamed gingiva. Extreme loss of bone support in 1978 radiographs.

inflammation need not extend to a periodontitis in most cases, even when the inflammation was present for extended periods in patients susceptible to periodontal disease.

5. The teeth that survived with greatest frequency were the mandibular canines and premolars. The teeth with narrow zones of attached gingiva include the resistant mandibular canines and premolars. Thus, the validity of the need for free gingival grafts prophylactically to widen the zone of attached gingiva is open to question.

6. Over a period of many years even those cases that had a downhill course exhibited a cyclic pattern of stability and destructive tendency. The periodontal attachment around one or a few teeth might be lost while the remainder of the dentition remained unchanged (Fig. 10-5). There is obviously an interplay between local

factors and general predisposition to disease, which is little understood. The period of instability usually began 4 to 5 years after treatment.

7. Among the patients in the downhill groups, a large number had cyanotic gingiva with little clinically obvious inflammation or enlargement. These patients most frequently developed heavy subgingival calculus deposits but had relatively little supragingival plaque.

8. Posttreatment tooth mobility, which was reduced from the mobility seen initially, was usually not destructive. Most cases in the study had some residual mobility that remained unchanged or decreased with time.

Recent research has provided support for the effectiveness of deep scaling procedures in both active treatment and maintenance of cases. In studies of the changes in bacterial flora and the histopathology of gingival inflammation subsequent to deep scaling of periodontal pockets, it was found that the bacterial flora was disrupted and required as much as 4 months for some organisms to reestablish themselves. The bacterial organisms reappeared in a distinct sequence, with the spirochetes and *Capnocytophaga* among the last to appear. The cells of the gingival inflammatory exudate also changed from being primarily plasma cells (the established lesion) to being primarily lymphocytes (developing lesion).

Those cases that exhibited further periodontal destruction during maintenance subsequent to the study were given tetracycline systemically as adjunctive therapy. The current investigations of the affect of tetracycline on the subgingival microflora indicate that scaling and tetracycline affect the organisms similarly and probably are synergistic initially.

References

Becker, W., et al. Untreated periodontal disease: A longitudinal study. J. Periodontol. 50:234, 1979.

Chace, R., et al. Subgingival curettage in periodontal therapy. J. Periodontol. 45:107, 1974.

Hirschfeld, L., et al. A long term survey of tooth loss in 600 treated periodontal patients. J. Periodontol. 49:225, 1978.

Knowles, J., et al. Comparison of results following three modalities of periodontal therapy related to tooth type and pocket depth. J. Clin. Periodontol. 7:32, 1980.

Ogilvie, A.L., et al. Recall and maintenance of the periodontal patient. Periodontics 5:198, 1967.

Parr, R.W., et al. Periodontal Maintenance Therapy. Berkeley, Calif.: Praxis Publ. Co., 1974.

Pihlstrom, B.L., et al. Comparison of surgical and non-surgical treatment of periodontal disease. J. Clin. Periodontol. 10:524, 1983.

Ramfjord, S.P., et al. Results of periodontal therapy related to tooth type. J. Periodontol. 51:270, 1980.

Ross, I.F., et al. A long term study of root retention in the treatment of maxillary molars with furcation involvements. J. Periodontol. 49:238, 1978.

Suomi, J.D., et al. The effect of controlled oral hygiene procedures on the progression of periodontal disease in adults. Results after third and final year. J. Periodontol. 42:152, 1971.

Chapter 11

Case Reports

Examples of long-term cases are helpful in realizing the potential effectiveness of deep scaling in the treatment of periodontal disease and maintenance of treated cases.

Two cases drawn from the records of Dr. Isidore Hirschfeld are included because of their longevity and the exclusive use of deep scaling and occlusal adjustment as the total therapy.

Case 1

Case 1 is a 28-year-old man who, in 1928, had "bleeding from the gums," drifting of the anterior teeth, and a generalized looseness of the teeth (Fig. 11-1a). On clinical examination, the gingiva exhibited an inflammatory enlargement, which had caused the drifting of the anterior teeth. Bone loss was moderately severe and generalized (Fig. 11-1b). Supragingival and subgingival calculus and plaque were heavy. Oral hygiene was poor. Pocket depths were in the 4- to 8-mm range.

Treatment

Treatment consisted of deep scaling, selective grinding, and home care instruction, including brushing with the Charter's method and the use of dental tape. The maintenance program consisted of one visit for deep scaling every 6 months. The patient was consistently effective in his home care, and maintenance visits were made regularly.

Results

Therapy resulted in eradication of inflammation, spontaneous repositioning of the migrated anterior teeth, stabilization of bone loss, and marked reduction of tooth mobility (Fig. 11-2a). Radiographs taken 40 years after initial treatment indicated that crestal bone had condensed with no further bone loss (Fig. 11-2b).

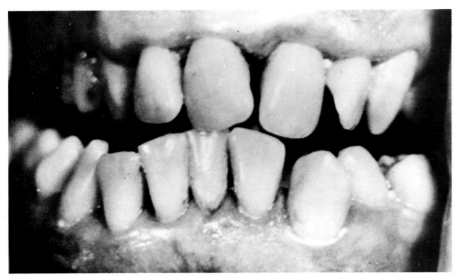

Figs. 11-1 a and b   Case 1, preoperative state.

Fig. 11-1a   Clinical photograph, 1928. Note diastemas between the maxillary central incisors and mandibular left lateral incisor and canine. Marginal gingival enlargement is present.

Fig. 11-1b   Radiographs, 1928. Extensive bone loss is evident throughout the dentition.

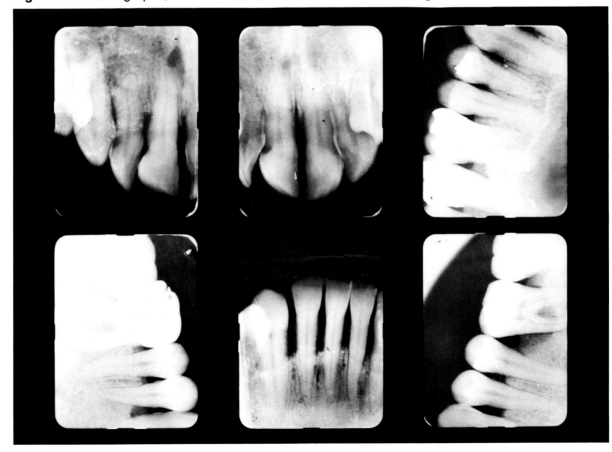

Figs. 11-2 a and b Case 1, postoperative state.

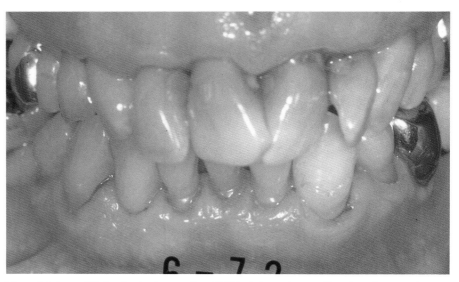

Fig. 11-2a Clinical photograph, 1972, taken immediately after maintenance deep scaling. The diastemas present in 1928 have closed, and gingival health is excellent.

Fig. 11-2b Radiographs, 1947, 19 years after original treatment, exhibit condensation of crestal bone with no further bone loss.

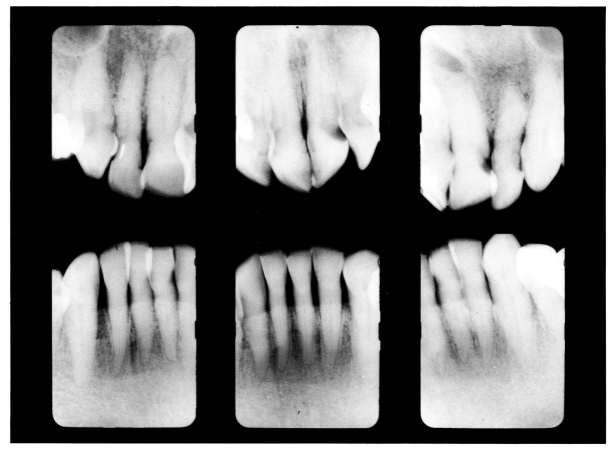

Case 2

Case 2 is a 33-year-old woman who, in 1925, had moderate to severe gingival inflammation, anterior tooth mobility, drifting, and severe bone loss (Fig. 11-3a). The lower anterior teeth were deemed hopeless, and extraction was advised (Fig. 11-3b). Since the patient preferred to maintain the teeth for as long as possible, the "hopeless" teeth were treated and maintained.

Treatment

Treatment consisted of deep scaling and selective tooth grinding. Home care instructions were repeated frequently because of the inability of the patient to execute the home care techniques effectively.

Results

Results of treatment included survival of the lower anterior teeth, with spontaneous repositioning to a moderate degree and some alveolar bone regrowth (Figs. 11-4a to c). During the 45 years of maintenance, the patient most frequently had moderate amounts of bacterial plaque and gingival inflammation (Fig. 11-4d). Maintenance visits were not consistently attended and averaged one or two annually.

Figs. 11-3 a and b   Case 2, pre-operative state.

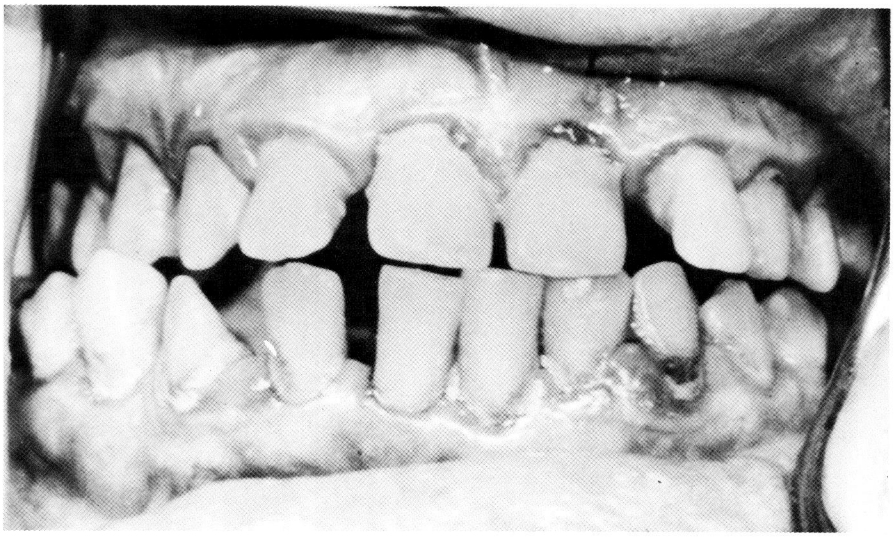

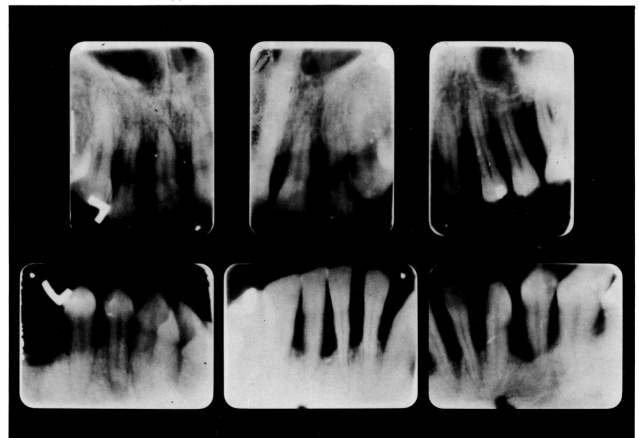

Fig. 11-3a   Clinical photograph, 1925, of heavy accumulations of plaque and calculus, with marginal gingival inflammation. Both maxillary and mandibular incisors have drifted facially.

Fig. 11-3b   Radiographs, 1925, exhibiting extensive bone loss. The mandibular incisors have lost almost all of their alveolar bone support.

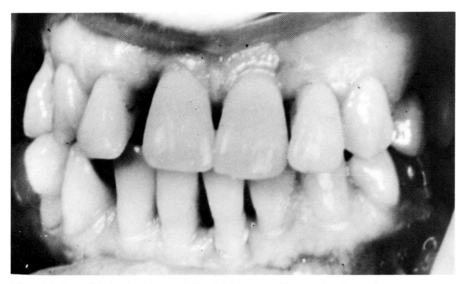

Figs. 11-4a to d Case 2, post-operative state.

Fig. 11-4a Clinical photograph, 1947, showing reduction of most diastemas and excellent gingival health.

Fig. 11-4b Radiographs, 1934, 9 years after treatment, indicating condensation of crestal bone and some bone regrowth.

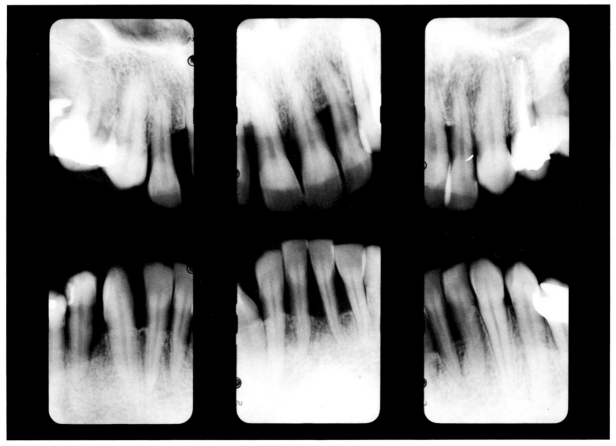

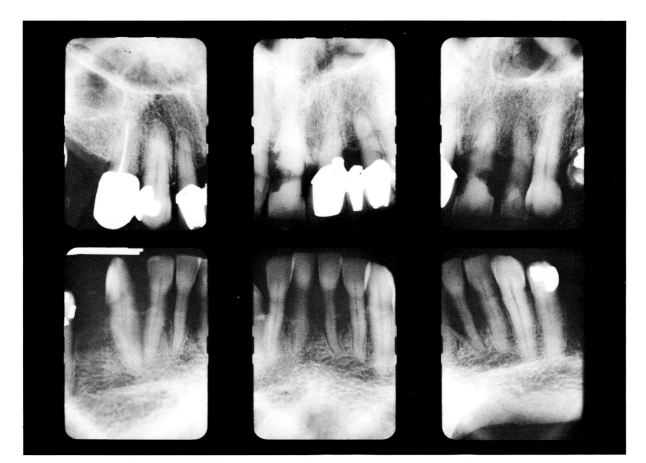

Fig. 11-4c Radiographs, 1972, 48 years after initial treatment. All the mandibular anterior teeth have survived, with some bone regrowth evident. The maxillary right lateral incisor was lost for endodontic reasons.

Fig. 11-4d Clinical photograph, 1972, showing presence of marginal inflammation and plaque and calculus accumulations.

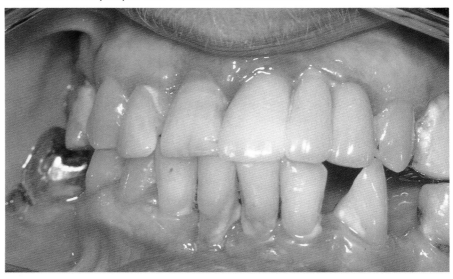

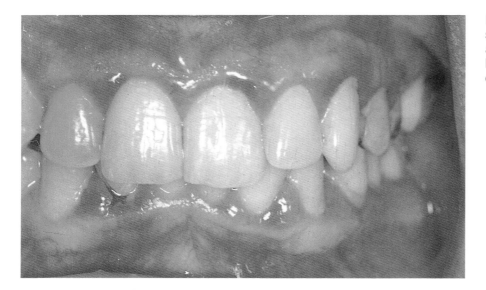

Fig. 11-5 Case 3, preoperative state. Clinical photograph at examination, 1956. Inflammatory hyperplasia of the gingiva is present generally.

Case 3

Case 3 is a 40-year-old man who, in 1954, had severe gingival inflammatory hyperplasia, spontaneous gingival bleeding, and generalized bone loss (Fig. 11-5). All the second molars were deemed highly questionable and were near to requiring extraction. The remaining molars had severe bone loss. Supragingival and subgingival calculus was heavy and spurlike. Mobilities were moderate but generalized. Moderate bacterial plaque accumulations were present in the posterior sextants and on the lingual surface of the mandibular anterior teeth.

Treatment

Treatment consisted of deep scaling and selective grinding. A gingivectomy was done on the maxillary left side, but the resultant tooth exposure was so uncomfortable that a similar procedure planned for the right side was never executed. Home care instructions included the use of dental floss. Some difficulty was encountered in passing the floss interproximally, thus limiting the patient's use of the floss.

Results

Results were good, with rapid resolution of gingival inflammation and reduction in pocket depth (Figs. 11-6a to d). Loss of the second molars occurred 10 years after initial treatment. Complete stabilization of the bone levels was evident, with some regrowth of alveolar bone in the anterior sextant. Because of crowding and an anterior synthetic restoration on the maxillary right canine and lateral incisor, a persistent local inflammation existed. Maintenance at 6-month intervals for 24 years was effective in stabilizing the condition. Occasional lapses in adequate home care caused severe gingivitis. Thus, the responsiveness of the gingival tissues to local plaque had not

Figs. 11-6a to h Case 3, preoperative and postoperative states.

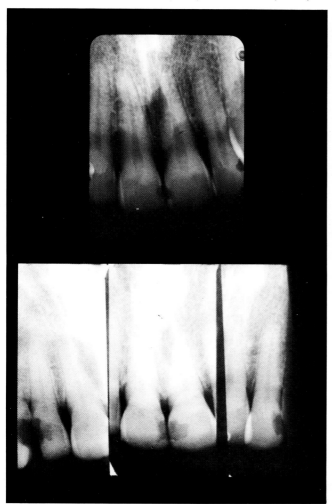

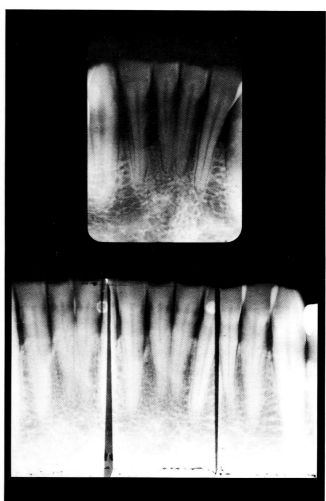

Fig. 11-6a Radiographs of maxillary incisors in 1956 *(top)* and 1976 *(bottom)*. Alveolar bone loss evident in 1956 seems to have leveled by either new attachment or a combination of new attachment and crestal bone resorption.

Fig. 11-6b Radiographs of mandibular incisors in 1956 *(top)* and 1976 *(bottom)*, showing similar positive changes as the maxillary incisors.

been changed by treatment and remained characteristic of the patient.

Of interest is the fact that, with time, it was difficult to see any difference in either pocket depths or degree of gingival recession when the surgically treated left maxillary posterior teeth were compared with the deep-scaled right posterior teeth (Figs. 11-6e to h).

In 1980, a granulation lesion developed distal to the maxillary right first premolar, with rapid alveolar bone loss. The lesion was treated by surgical excision, after which the bone level stabilized.

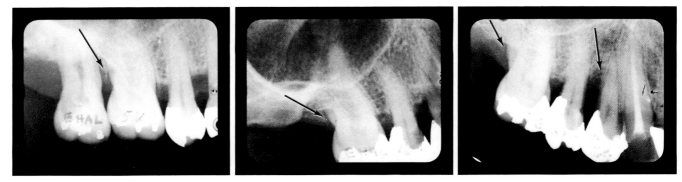

Fig. 11-6c Radiographs in 1958 *(left),* 1976 *(center),* and 1980 *(right),* showing loss of the maxillary right second molar but stabilization of the bone levels on the distal of the first molar. Rapid bone loss occurred in 1980 distal to the first premolar as a result of a rapidly developed granulation tissue lesion.

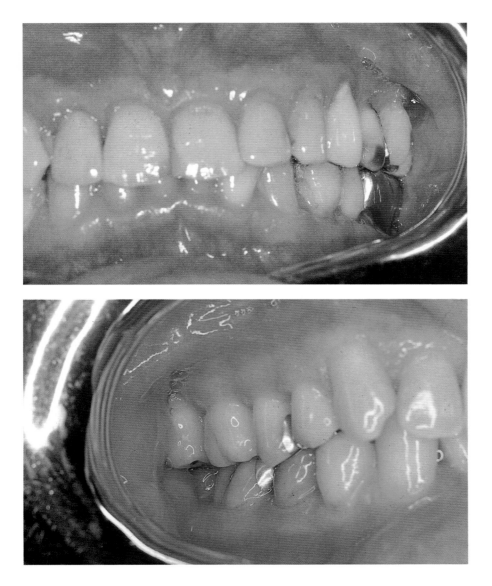

Fig. 11-6d Clinical photograph, 1980, 24 years after initial treatment. Gingival health is excellent with the exception of the maxillary right canine–lateral papilla and the lower central incisor.

Fig. 11-6e Clinical photograph, 1958, of the right side treated by deep scaling, exhibiting only slight gingival recession.

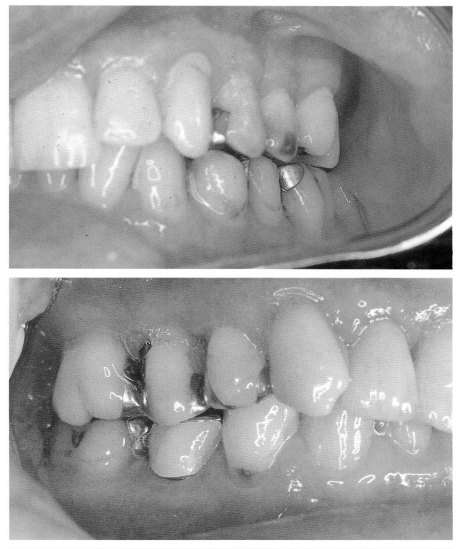

Fig. 11-6f Clinical photograph, 1958, of the left side treated by gingival resection. Moderate gingival recession is present.

Fig. 11-6g Clinical photograph, 1980, of right side.

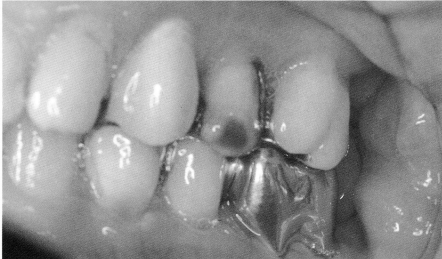

Fig. 11-6h Clinical photograph, 1980, of left side, showing gingival regrowth and similar contours to the deep-scaled right side.

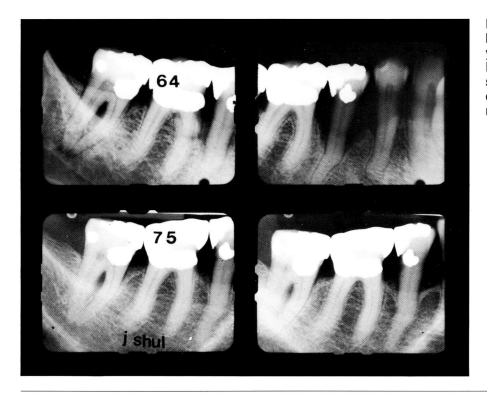

Fig. 11-7 Case 4. Radiographs before treatment (1964) and 11 years after treatment (1975). Note regrowth of bone around the second premolar and the stability of bone levels on the second molar.

Case 4

Case 4 is a 55-year-old woman who, in 1964, had a history of recurrent periodontal abscesses. All missing teeth were lost for periodontal reasons. Periodontal pocketing was severe, but there was no patterned distribution. The gingiva was slightly inflamed, with moderately heavy, platelike subgingival calculus. Oral hygiene was good. All molars had furcation involvements, with the most severe being the lower right second molar.

Treatment

Treatment consisted of deep scaling preparatory to surgical flap procedures. Full-thickness mucoperiosteal flaps were laid and all root surfaces scaled and bony deformities debrided. Maintenance was at 3-month intervals.

Results

Pocket reduction was partially effective, with some residual pocket depth present in the molar areas. Bone regrowth around the mandibular right second premolar was evident. The pocket depth on the mandibular right second molar was only slightly lessened and extended well into a Class II furcation involvement. The maintenance program was effective in preventing further bone loss over a period of 21 years. The bone regrowth around the premolar was retained (Fig. 11-7).

Figs. 11-8a and b Case 5, pre-operative state.

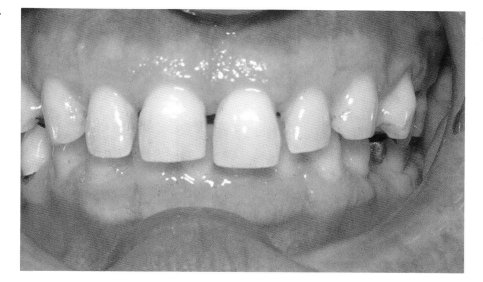

Fig. 11-8a Clinical photographs, 1968. Thick gingiva masks the inflammation of the deep pocket on the maxillary left central incisor. Only a slight cyanotic alteration of the gingival color is evident.

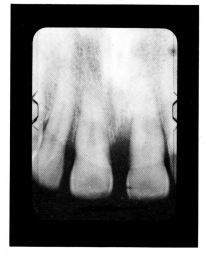

Fig. 11-8b Radiograph, 1966, indicating considerable alveolar bone loss about the maxillary left central incisor.

Case 5

Case 5 is a 43-year-old man who, on initial examination, had loose maxillary anterior teeth, with thick slightly cyanotic gingiva overlying deep proximal and palatal pockets. Moderate pocket depth was present elsewhere. The left maxillary central incisor had drifted labially as a result of extensive bone loss and external forces (Figs. 11-8a and b). Subgingival calculus was moderately heavy; plaque accumulations were slight.

The patient was a professional musician (clarinetist), who applied pressure to the anterior teeth with the mouthpiece of the instrument.

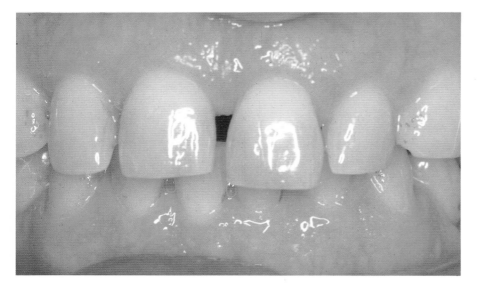

Figs. 11-9a and b Case 5, postoperative state.

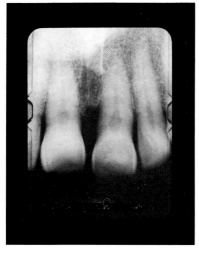

Fig. 11-9a Clinical photograph, 1980, showing that little gingival recession occurred during treatment and the 14 years of maintenance.

Fig. 11-9b Radiograph, 1980, showing some bone regrowth on the maxillary central incisor in spite of parafunctional pressure.

Treatment

Since no changes in the configuration of the anterior gingiva were acceptable because of possible consequences to the patient's ability to play the instrument, surgical periodontal procedures were contraindicated. Repeated deep scaling was the treatment for the whole dentition. The maxillary central incisor was moved palatally using a Hawley bite plane. Home care was stressed, and the patient became very proficient in plaque control.

Results

Reattachment of the periodontal fibers seemed to have occurred on the maxillary left central incisor, as evidenced by alveolar bone regrowth (Figs. 11-9a and b). Maintenance for 16 years by scaling at 6-month intervals maintained the attachment in spite of the pressure applied to the tooth during playing of the instrument. In recent years, the use of the maxillary retainer has been sporadic, causing a slight relapse in the position of the tooth.

Comparison of cases

These cases illustrate the application of deep scaling and root planing in active therapy and during maintenance. Cases 1 and 2 were of the highly proliferative type, with a distinct relationship between etiologic agents and tissue response. This case type responds superbly to deep scaling and should be treatment planned accordingly. Case 3 was of the same type but was under active treatment when surgical treatment was the vogue, thus, the gingivectomy in one quadrant. Because it exhibited inflammatory hyperplasia, the case could well have been treated by deep scaling alone.

Case 4 had deep pockets and only slight gingival inflammation and would, therefore, respond only modestly to definitive deep scaling. In the posterior segments, the flap procedures, typical of the time, produced the expected gingival changes. The anterior teeth were treated by deep scaling alone. Regular maintenance by deep scaling stabilized the periodontium during a long period of observation. The case represents the usual combination of active therapies used in most instances.

Case 5 is essentially one in which the unexpected occurred. With advanced disease affecting three surfaces, the central incisor responded to deep scaling by regeneration of the periodontium. This regeneration occurred in spite of the continued trauma by the clarinet mouthpiece. The fact that the tooth was single rooted and easily accessible to scaling were important factors in the success of treatment.

Though deep scaling will play a varied role in the active treatment of periodontal disease, its primacy in maintenance is unequivocal.

Index

A

Albucasis 39, 64
Alveolar bone,
  destruction of 24, 25, 29, 31, 32, 35
  effects of plaque on 17
  immune response 23
Alveolar process, anatomical variations 11, 13
  effect on gingiva 11, 56
  thickness and infrabony defects 58

B

Bacteria,
  subgingival 27, 28
  supragingival 27

C

Calculus,
  and periodontitis 44, 45
  development of 16, 17, 27
  gingival reaction to 40, 42, 43, 45
  subgingival 27, 28, 29, 46
    tenacity and amount 113, 114
    thin, smooth 115
  supragingival 28
Case reports 143–157
Cementum pathology 30
Charting, for treatment planning 134
Curettage, soft tissue 97, 98

D

Dental restorations, gingival inflammation 50
Disease range variations 11–38

E

Epithelium, junctional, oral, sulcular 11–12

F

Flap surgery 154
Food impaction, gingival inflammation 50
Frenum 11, 15
Furcation,
  scaling 116
  treatment planning 133

G

Gingiva,
  anatomical variations 11
  attached 11, 12, 15
  cyanosis 41, 44
  discoloration 26, 27
  disease progression 18, 21–27
  effects of plaque on 16
  immune response 23
  inflammation 17, 18, 19, 22, 26
    from dental restorations 50
    from food impaction 50
    from mouth breathing 50
    masked 41, 43
  keratinized 11, 12
  marginal 11, 15
  normal 11, 16
  reaction to calculus 40, 42, 43, 45
  reaction to plaque 40, 42, 43, 45
  recession 43, 60, 130
    generalized 128
  stippled 11, 12, 14
  thickness variations 11, 12, 13
Gingival groove, free 12, 15
Gingival hyperplasia 21
  phenytoin-induced, scaling 55
Gingival sulcus,
  anatomical variations 12
  ecology of 23
  suppuration from 47
  tissue response 23
Gingivitis, 17, 31
  acute necrotizing ulcerative 31, 32, 34
  definitive deep scaling failures 56
  desquamative, scaling 55
  marginal,
    definitive deep scaling 49
    etiology 49, 50, 51

necrotizing ulcerative, scaling | 51
Granulation lesion, | 33, 34, 35
   treatment of | 60
Grinding, selective | 150

H

Hawley bite plane | 156
Health, range variations | 11–38
Hepatitis, serum | 77
Hutchinson, R. G. | 39

I

Idiopathic fibromatosis, scaling | 55
Instrumentation principles | 91
Instruments,
  chisel,
    prophylaxis | 64, 65
     Zerfing | 64, 66, 73
  curette | 64, 68, 70, 79
    Goldman-Fox 3 | 73, 74, 115, 120
    Gracey | 68, 69, 70, 72, 73, 74, 89, 90
     | 115, 116, 118
    McCall | 71, 72, 73, 74, 115, 117, 118, 120
  file | 67, 79, 81, 82
    Hirschfeld | 68, 73, 74, 82, 91, 95, 119
    Zerfing | 79
  flat-edged | 78
  infection from | 77
  maintenance | 76–83
  planing | 63–75
  scaler | 79, 80
    Hoe | 66, 67
    pick | 64, 65
      Darby-Perry sickle | 64, 65
      Jacquette | 64, 65
      McCall | 64
    ultrasonic | 75
  scaling | 63–75
  sharpening | 76–83
  whittler blade, Neivert | 78, 81, 82
Interdental,
  col | 15
  saddle | 15
  space, scaling | 119
    bone width and pathology | 124, 132
Interradicular space, scaling | 119

J

Juvenile periodontitis | 29, 30, 33
  patterns of disease | 34

L

Labial frenum | 15
Lichen planus, erosive, scaling | 55

M

Maintenance care, | 137–142
  long-term | 140, 141, 143, 146, 150, 154
Mouth breathing, gingival inflammation | 50
Mucosa, alveolar | 15

P

Pain,
  analgesia for | 123
  causes | 121
  control | 121–123
  hypnosis for | 123
  posttreatment | 123
  topical anesthesia for | 122
Papilla,
  hyperplastic | 21
  interdental | 11, 15, 32
    inflammation | 16, 17
Periodontal abscess, | 32, 34, 54
  treatment of | 54, 55
Periodontal disease,
  bacteriology | 27
  destruction by | 24, 25
  developmental stages | 18, 21–27
  distribution affected teeth | 26, 128
  individual susceptibility | 26
  treatment objectives | 39
  types | 31
Periodontal pockets,
  definitive deep scaling | 40, 46, 53, 57, 58, 59
  masked | 26, 41, 43
  on molars | 115, 116, 117
  on narrow roots | 119

Periodontitis,
    absence of gingival inflammation   56
    adult   32
    calculus in   44, 45
    deep scaling   40, 45
    definitive deep scaling   52, 53, 57
    gingival inflammation   44
    juvenile (periodontosis)   29, 30, 33
    marginal   19
    masked   43
    oversized teeth in   43
    tooth surfaces affected   131, 132
Periodontium,
    anatomical variations   11
    maintenance care   137–142
    normal   11, 16
Planing,
    areas of difficulty   113–120
    instrument choice   98
    instrument grasp   84, 85
    long sessions   96
    positions for   98–112
    rests   88, 89
    strokes   85, 86, 92–96, 97
    techniques   84–112
Plaque,
    accumulation   18, 19
    development of   16
    effects on gingiva   16, 17, 18, 40, 42, 43, 45
    subgingival bacteria   27
    supragingival bacteria   27

R

Radiographs, in treatment
    planning   124–130, 134
Recall care   137
Riggs, John   39
Root surface pathology, treatment   30

S

The Sayings of Pythagoras on Scaling
    the Teeth with Iron Instruments   39
Scaling,
    areas of difficulty   113–120
    deep,
        as sole therapy   61, 143, 146, 155

    history of   39
    objectives   39–48
    of periodontal pockets   46
    predictions of change from   45
deep definitive   39
    case report   143, 146
    cases amenable to   49–56
    failures   56–61
    for desquamative gingivitis   55
    for erosive lichen planus   55
    for idiopathic fibromatosis   55
    for marginal gingivitis   49
    for necrotizing gingivitis   51
    for periodontal abscess   54
    for periodontal pockets   40, 53, 57, 58, 59
    for periodontitis   52, 53, 57
    for phenytoin-induced gingival
        hyperplasia   55
    predictable results   49–62
drifted or inclined teeth   120
furcations   116, 117
instrument choice   98
instrument grasp   84, 85
interdental space   119
interradicular space   119
long sessions   96
molar periodontal pockets   115, 116, 117
narrow-rooted teeth   119
    positions for   98–112
    rests   88, 89
    strokes   85, 86, 92–96, 97
    techniques   84–112
    tooth line angles   117, 118
    ultrasonic   97
Suppuration   47

T

Teeth,
    distribution of affected   128
    drifted, scaling   120
    inclined, scaling   120
    surfaces affected   131, 132
Tooth loss, distribution of   138, 139
Tooth mobility, treatment planning   133
Treatment planning,
    charting   134
    choice of   124–136
    plan formulation   135
    radiographs in   124–130, 134
    sequence   124–136